English
Tea & Cakes

METRO BOOKS
New York

An Imprint of Sterling Publishing
387 Park Avenue South
New York, NY 10016

ISBN 978-1-4351-4632-7

For information about custom editions, special sales,
and premium and corporate purchases, please contact
Sterling Special Sales at 800-805-5489 or
specialsales@sterlingpublishing.com.

Manufactured in China

2 4 6 8 10 9 7 5 3 1

www.sterlingpublishing.com

English Tea & Cakes

METRO BOOKS
New York

Contents

Introduction

Come in, sit down, and pour yourself a refreshing cup of the finest tea. This book has everything you ever wanted to know about English afternoon tea and cake—together with over 100 delicious recipes so you can host your very own afternoon tea party. Find out about the many different types of tea available and how best to serve them, as well as other essential accompaniments such as preserves (or jam, as the British like to call it).

From classic cakes to bite-size treats and superb scones to tantalizing teabreads, there are delicious baked goods to suit every taste. Try your hand at regional classics such as Bara Brith, Bath Buns or Banbury Cakes, or go one step further and make your own delicious fruit jams to go with any of the tempting scone recipes.

Follow the great advice on hosting your own tea party, check out the straightforward golden rules for successful baking, choose a handful of delicious recipes and you'll be well on your way to creating an occasion worthy of the Queen herself.

The Art of Afternoon Tea

Fancy a Cuppa?

The wide variety of teas available today means that each individual tea-drinker can choose something to suit the palate, time of day, food being served, mood, season and weather.

Everyone has a favorite early-morning tea, a tea to drink by the fire on a dark and dismal winter afternoon, an evening tea to enjoy after a wonderful dinner. There are no firm rules as to which tea should be drunk when, but here are some helpful guidelines:

First thing in the morning and at breakfast choose a strong black tea that gives a good dose of caffeine and helps get the brain and body going, such as English Breakfast, Irish Breakfast, Assam, Kenya or Yunnan. These teas all have a strength and depth that marry well with the strong flavors of cooked breakfast foods and with breads and pastries served with preserves or honey.

Mid-morning and at lunchtime choose a tea that will continue to help you concentrate and perform well through the working day. Any of the morning teas work well, or choose smoky Lapsang Souchong, flavorful Ceylon, China Keemun or Nilgiri. If lunch consists of oriental food, choose a green Sencha or Chinese Chun Mee or Gunpowder.

As the afternoon progresses turn to lighter teas that offer a fragrance and gentleness to soothe and calm—perhaps a peachy oolong, a fruity Darjeeling, a lighter Ceylon, any variety of green tea, or a flavored tea such as mango or peach.

At afternoon tea choose teas that pair well with the food offered. Earl Grey goes extremely well with cheese sandwiches or savories, and with lemon cake or lemon tarts; Darjeeling is excellent with anything creamy so is perfect with scones and clotted cream; Lapsang Souchong is wonderful with smoked salmon or smoked chicken sandwiches; a brisk Ceylon enhances fresh fruit or sandwiches made with cucumber, tomatoes and other salad ingredients; strong Kenya blends are great with chocolate cakes and rich truffles.

In the evening perfect teas are the lighter oolongs, greens and whites. These are very cleansing after a meal and offer an elegance and cleanness that is good after dinner and before sleep. These are also teas that drink well alone, without food, and create just the right mood for the time of day when life begins to slow down. The evenig is also a great time to sip herbal infusions such as camomile or mint.

Equipment for preparing tea

The teapot
The teapots used in the West today developed from the little round-bodied teapots that were imported from China to Europe and North America on the same ships that brought the tea. Whereas coffee pots have always been tall and usually straight-sided, teapots have retained their low, squat shape. The early imported pots were small because that is how the Chinese made and used their pots (and indeed still use them today), but as the cost of tea in Europe fell during the 18th and 19th centuries and tea became more of an everyday beverage, teapots grew in size.

Choosing a teapot
The best teapots are those made in glazed stoneware, pottery, china, porcelain and glass. Silver tewares have been popular since the late 17th century but silver does not necessarily make the best brewing vessel. Silver can hold the flavor of the last tea brewed in it and so needs very careful washing and rinsing after use.

Caring for your teapot
Teapots that are glazed inside can be washed in a dishwasher or by hand using normal dishwashing detergents. However, to be sure that the flavor of brewed tea is not tainted with residues of soap, always rinse the teapot very carefully. To restore a tea's flavor and aroma to a pot, spoon in a scoop of dry tea leaves, place the lid on the pot and leave to stand until the next time it is used, then empty out the dry leaves before the pot is re-used. To , remove tea stains from the inside and spout of a teapot, measure in two large spoonfuls of baking soda, fill the pot with boiling water and leave to soak overnight. Rinse thoroughly and dry.

Yixing teapots
Yixing is famous for its many colored clays and for the teapots made from them. Since the 1500s, potters in this Chinese lakeside town have been fashioning the most exquisite unglazed teapots in the form of houses, lotus flowers, pumpkins, Buddhist priests, boxes, bundles of bamboo, dragons, fruit, vegetables, human figures and buildings. Yixing pots are said to be the best brewing vessels for oolong teas and because the interior of the pot is unglazed, each pot must only be used for one tea. Over time, the pot absorbs the flavor of the tea and builds up a patina that enhances future brews. For this reason, a Yixing pot should never be washed with detergents but should simply be rinsed and allowed to dry.

British Tea

For over a decade, tea has been growing in the warm, balmy climate of the Tregothnan Estate in Cornwall, at the extreme south-western tip of Britain. Since 1335, the vast estate has belonged to the Boscawen family and the interest in unusual and exotic plants has been handed down through the generations. Ornamental camellias (Camellia japonica) have been grown in the open here for two hundred years and the first experimental seedlings of the tea bush (Camellia sinensis) were planted at Tregothnan in the mid-nineties. An old saying states that "Cornwall doesn't have a winter, just a languid spring!" and with temperatures always a little higher than in other parts of Britain, it can feel rather like the higher regions of Darjeeling.

In 1999, 20 acres of sheltered valley were cleared and the first seedlings, imported from various tea-growing regions around the world, were planted out and since then a new section of the estate has been cleared and planted to increase the total area to 30 acres. The estate produces both green and black teas and an Earl Grey flavored with the citrus fruit bergamot which is also grown at Tregothnan. The best of the teas are usually produced in the late spring.

Infuser and plunger teapots

The flavor of tea can become very unpleasant if the leaves stand for too long in the hot water, so many different pots are now available that contain their own purpose-designed infuser basket that can be lifted out, or that have a plunger that allows the separation of the tea from the liquor once the tea has brewed. When choosing a pot with an inbuilt infuser, make sure that the infuser basket or bag is large enough to allow the leaves to move around, swell up and release their color and flavor into the water, and check that the design allows the lid to sit neatly on the top of the pot both when the infuser is in the pot and after it has been lifted out. If you are choosing a plunger pot, make sure that the plunger really does separate the leaves from the water. As long as any of the leaves are in contact with the water, the tea will go on brewing.

Infusers

Also available is a range of plastic, metal, cloth and paper infusers that allow the easy separation of the leaf from the water. Aluminum is not a good choice for these infusers as it taints the flavor of the tea, but chrome, porcelain, nylon, plastic, unbleached paper are all excellent—as long as they are large enough to allow the tea to brew properly. They should be designed so that they fit down into the bottom of the teapot, are easy to handle and easy to lift out once the tea has brewed. Infuser mugs are also available. These act like a mini teapot and are a useful alternative in the workplace.

The guywan

The Guywan is one of China's traditional brewing vessels. It consists of a deep bowl that has no handle, a lid and a saucer. The loose tea leaves are measured into the guywan, water is added and, with the lid in place, the leaves are allowed to brew. The liquor is then drunk from the cup while the lid is carefully angled to hold the leaves back inside the cup.

There are multiple ways to brew tea, but ultimately you should choose a method that works best for you—the last thing that making tea should be is stressful or difficult! If you can borrow a teapot, infuser or guywan from friends or family then do so, and try them all out before investing in your own equipment.

Japanese tea bowls

The large, rather rough, handmade pottery bowls used for whisked tea during the Japanese Tea Ceremony have been made in the same way since the Japanese started drinking tea almost 1,200 years ago. They are thought to have developed from Korean rice bowls and, since most potters in Japan at that time came from Korea, it was this style that was adapted for tea-drinking vessels. The bowls must be of a certain thickness; if they are too thin they will be too hot to hold and may allow the tea to cool too rapidly. Conversely, bowls that are too thick will not become sufficiently hot.

Tea hotplates

Several companies now offer glass or metal hotplates on which to keep brewed tea warm. These should never be too hot and the little candle lights (or tea lights) designed for use in them are ideal. However, tea kept warm in this way will deteriorate after about 25 minutes and be sure never to stand a pot of tea on one of these special burners if the leaves are still in the pot.

Tea cosies

Tea cosies are useful for keeping a pot of tea warm but should never be used if the tea leaves are still in the pot, as the tea may become bitter and unpleasant.

Caddy spoons and scoops

The ideal measure for spooning tea from caddy or packet to pot holds approximately $1/8$ oz. The perfect measure for most teas is $1/8$ oz of tea to $3/4$ cup of water. This varies according to the type of tea used and personal taste.

Milk in tea

In the early days of tea-drinking in Britain, milk was not a regular addition to the cup. The custom seems to have started at the end of the 17th century and perhaps developed because milk and cream were found to soften the slightly bitter taste of tea. The habit of course raises an important question—should the milk be poured into the tea or the tea into the milk? The answer depends on class, region, style of brewing and, of course, personal taste! Some will say that etiquette demands that the milk should be added to the tea and argue that it is more genteel and allows control of color and strength, etc. (It is true that in the upper circles of Victorian society, poured cups of tea were handed to guests by the hostess or servants and the guests asked to help themselves to milk or cream and sugar.) Those in favor of "milk in first" claim that this makes for a better mixing of the two fluids. There is also a belief that if cold milk is poured into boiling tea, there is a slight risk of spoiling the flavor of the brew by caramelizing the fat in the milk. Scientific experiments have in fact shown that this can happen and also that tiny globules of fat from the milk can remain floating on the surface of the cup of tea. But there is no easy answer to this point of debate and each individual tea-drinker must decide which method is best.

Tea Drinking

Drinking tea in Britain is a ritual that has its origins in the mid-17th century when tea started to arrive via Holland and Portugal. Merchants and aristocrats imported small amounts of tea into Britain in the 1650s, but it was Charles II's marriage in 1662 to a Portuguese princess, Catherine of Braganza, that established tea drinking as an accepted practice.

of the majority of the population until 1784, when the tax was reduced from 119 percent to 12 percent and tea overtook gin and ale in the popularity stakes. Had the tax remained, it is likely that the British would have ended up drinking coffee like the French and Germans.

In the first half of the 18th century a powerful campaign against the coffee houses, which had become bawdy dens of iniquity, succeeded in closing them down, and, in their place, the pleasure gardens at Vauxhall, Chelsea, Marylebone, Islington, Bermondsey, Kentish Town and Kilburn provided family entertainment in London. The price of entry to these gardens sometimes included tea with bread and butter, the idea being that, after enjoying rides on the river, horse-riding, listening to music or wandering through beautifully

Regular consignments were soon being ordered for the King and Queen and tea drinking became a fashionable activity. Meanwhile, enterprising merchants, keen to increase sales of this new commodity, engaged in elaborate advertising campaigns, and gradually the trend spread. Tea was served, and loose tea sold, in the coffee houses that

had sprung up in London and some provincial towns in the 1650s, but the high tax levied by King Charles II meant that it was very expensive and therefore out of the reach of the working classes. Ale and gin continued to be the standard drinks

Afternoon Tea

Afternoon tea is said to have been "invented" in the early 19th century by Anna, wife of the 7th Duke of Bedford. Breakfast in those days was taken at nine or ten o'clock in the morning, and dinner, which had previously been eaten at two or three o'clock in the afternoon, was not until eight or nine o'clock. By four o'clock the Duchess, and no doubt others too, felt a little peckish; she therefore asked her footman to bring her all her tea-making equipage to her private room so that she could brew herself a pot of tea and enjoy it with a little light refreshment. The Duchess was so pleased with this arrangement that she started inviting her friends to join her, and soon all of London's elegant society was sipping "afternoon tea" and gossiping all the while about people, places and events. With their tea they nibbled dainty sandwiches or neat slices of light sponge cake flavored with candied orange or lemon peel, or caraway seeds.

In the late nineteenth century tea was actively sold to the middle classes; it was no longer an exclusively aristocratic or upper-class beverage.

Teas are blended by the major companies to offer tea that tastes the same in every box.

tended gardens, the family could relax and take some refreshment together. Sadly, the gardens survived for only a short time; by 1850 most had closed, but not before the ritual of afternoon tea had been firmly established as part of the British way of life.

In 1884 the activities of the manageress of the London Bridge branch of the Aerated Bread Company (the ABC) brought afternoon tea out of the elegant salons of the aristocracy and into the realm of everyday middle- and working-class people. This enterprising lady, who was in the habit of offering a cup of tea and a chat to her regular customers when they came in to buy their loaves of bread, persuaded her employers to allow her to create a public tearoom on the premises. Other companies quickly followed suit and soon every high street had its ABC, Express Dairy, Lyons' or Kardomah tearoom. By the 1920s going out to tea was a pastime enjoyed by people from all classes and walks of life. Children who grew up during the Edwardian period have fond memories of tea out with nanny, and most people remember their favorite tearooms with nostalgia and pleasure.

The fashion for tea gradually dwindled, and the tea shops were replaced by fast-food chains. In the mid-1980s, however, there was a revival of interest: new tea shops opened in unlikely places and quickly became popular; a rash of books about tea including teatime recipes appeared on bookstore shelves; tea dances again became the rage, even in provincial hotels and village halls; and going out for afternoon tea is now very much back in fashion.

Tea dances of the 1930s were a great place to show off the fashions of the day.

The Tea Dance

In the grander hotels and restaurants, tea dances became the craze from about 1912 onwards. A demonstration of the tango, which originated in the back streets of Buenos Aires, was given first in Paris and then in London. Initially couples danced between the restaurant tables, but, as the idea caught on, a space was cleared in the middle of the floor. Soon tango-teas and matinees were being held in most hotels and in half a dozen theatres around London. Books were written telling society hostesses how to organize tea dances, restaurants started tango-clubs, and dance teachers, such as Victor Silvester, made their fortunes. One well-known teacher of the time—Miss Gladys Beattie Crozier—wrote in her book *The Tango and How to Dance It*:

"What could be pleasanter on a dull wintry afternoon, at 5 o'clock or so, when calls or shopping are over, than to drop into one of the cheery little Thé Dansant clubs ... to take one's place at a tiny table ... to enjoy a most elaborate and delicious tea served within a moment of one's arrival, while listening to an excellent string band playing delicious haunting airs".

The Tea Bush

There are easily more than 10,000 different teas made around the world in more than 35 different countries. Yet all of them are made from the leaves and leaf buds of the tea bush, more properly called the Camellia sinensis, a relative of the Camellia japonica that we grow in our gardens as a decorative shrub with beautiful flowers. There are two main varieties that are used to make tea—the Camellia sinensis, a native of China, and the Camellia sinensis var. assamica, a native of Assam in north-east India. From these two varieties there are about

600 cultivars that have resulted from cross-breeding over the centuries. Each of these grows differently depending on local conditions and each resulting tea will have a different character.

The many different types of tea are separated according to their manufacture, and the main categories are white, green, oolong and black.

White teas are made from the tightly furled buds of a particular varietal of the tea bush which pushes out plump buds covered with silvery-white hairs. After plucking, the buds are dried in the sun and packed.

Green teas are made from the leaves and leaf buds of the tea bush which, after picking, are either steamed or pan-fried to de-enzyme the leaf and then rolled or shaped by hand or machine. Some green teas have needle-like leaves that are dark green, flat and shiny.

Gunpowder tea is made by rolling each leaf into a tiny tight ball that looks like a little pellet of lead shot, hence the name "gunpowder tea".

Oolong teas are made by gently shaking or lightly rolling freshly picked and withered leaves and then allowing them to oxidize for a short time before drying.

Black teas are made by picking, withering, rolling or chopping the green leaf before allowing it to fully oxidize until it turns to a very deep amber brown. Drying in hot ovens removes almost all but 2–3% of the remaining water and the tea is sorted and packed, ready for delivery to the stores and supermarkets.

British Favorites

The most commonly drunk teas in the UK are Darjeeling with its lightly astringent, muscatel quality, Assam with a warm, woody, malty character, Ceylon teas from the island of Sri Lanka with their bright, brisk, golden flavor, English Breakfast-style teas that are made from Assam, Ceylon and African teas, and offer a depth of flavor that marries well with strongly flavored foods, smoky Lapsang Souchong from China, and Earl Grey, tea flavored with essential oil of bergamot. Although in Britain we traditionally add milk and sometimes sugar to our tea, many teas taste much better drunk without.

Any white, green, oolong or black tea can be flavored with fruits, flowers, and herbs to make flavored or scented teas. Other popular "teas" in Britain are infusions made from fruit, spices and herbs that don't include the leaves of the tea bush, such as mint or camomile.

Naming the drink

In English, it is tea, but once upon a time, it was tee or tay. In India it is cha or chai. How did the different words develop? The form of the name that entered each language depended on the route by which tea was first traded into that country. When tea first traveled outside China to the Arab countries and Russia, the Mandarin word, cha, spread with the goods. In Persian, Japanese and Hindi, the word settled as cha, in Arabic, shai, in Tibetan, ja, in Turkish, chay and in Russian, chai. When the Portuguese first started buying tea from the Chinese, they traded through the port of Macao where the Mandarin word for tea had become ch'a in the locally spoken Cantonese. But Dutch tea ships sailed in and out of the port of Amoy in China's Fujian Province and so used the local Amoy word te, pronounced "tay", and changed it to thee. As it was the Dutch who were mainly responsible for trading tea to other European countries and beyond, the oriental beverage became known as tea or tee in English; thé in French; thee in German; te in Italian, Spanish, Danish, Norwegian, Hungarian, and Malay; tee in Finnish; tey in Tamil; thay in Singhalese; and Thea to scientists.

Brewing Tea

The first important decision to be made when choosing a tea is whether to buy teabags or loose leaf. Many people prefer teabags because they are easier to handle, the quantity of tea is already measured out, they do not present the problem of how to dispose of the wet leaves, they allow for the easy removal of the bag from the brew once the correct strength has been achieved and are generally convenient and quick to use.

Some teabags are extremely disappointing because of the small amount and poor quality of the leaf inside the bag. However, there are companies that do offer very good teabags containing quality leaf. The latest trend is for bags made of nylon gauze (often referred to as "crystal') or muslin. As well as being extremely sophisticated and stylish, these bags usually contain larger grades of leaf and allow the tea enough room to swell up and release its flavor and color more successfully into the water. Many true tea connoisseurs intensely dislike the idea of teabags and prefer always to choose a loose leaf. The advantages, as they see it, are that a much wider selection of loose-leaf teas is available from around the world, the brewer can decide what quantity and quality of tea to use, loose tea almost always gives a better, more subtle and fuller-flavored brew than teabags.

For the connoisseur, the ritual of measuring out the leaves into the pot is an important part of the tea-brewing ceremony.

Tea-leaf reading

For hundreds of years, the art of tea-leaf reading has fascinated and entranced tea-drinkers. Many people believe that the wet tea leaves scattered in the cup after the tea has been drunk are as good a guide to future events as the reading of palms and tarot cards. Tasseology is an intuitive art married with psychic skills that enables the reader to see into the future. The information gained from a tea-leaf reading usually applies only to the 24 hours immediately following the reading and for the best results, the reader must only look for answers to specific questions. A reading is only relevant to whoever has drunk from the cup.

- To prepare the cup, make a pot of tea in the usual way. Larger leaves are best as they create a more revealing mixture of images and patterns.
- Pour a cup of tea without using a strainer, so that some of the leaves go into the cup with the liquor.
- Drink the tea in the usual way but leave about a teaspoonful of liquid in the bottom of the cup with the leaves.

The drinker then holds the cup in the left hand with the rim upwards and turns it fast three times in an anticlockwise direction. The drinker tips the cup onto a saucer and allows the tea to drain into the saucer before turning the cup the right way up again and handing it to the reader. The reader holds the cup with the handle pointing towards the body and tries to interpret the significance of the leaves, and so help the drinker relate the pattern to specific aspects of their life—and to the specific question being asked.

The case for teabags or loose tea

Advantages of teabags

- easy to brew just one cup
- quick and convenient
- easy to separate tea from liquor once the brew has reached the correct strength
- no untidy wet leaves to dispose of
- useful for brewing large quantities of tea for special events, etc.

Disadvantages of most types of teabags

- do not offer the wide selection of world teas that are available as loose tea
- contain small particles of tea that brew quickly but often lack subtlety of flavor (nylon gauze bags do now allow larger grades of leaf to be bagged)
- often do not allow the tea enough room to brew properly
- the paper of the teabag stops the full flavor of the tea infusing out into the water
- teabags lose their flavor and quality more quickly than loose-leaf tea
- only small-leafed teas can be put into most types of teabag

Advantages of loose-leaf tea

- the consumer has an endless choice of world teas
- deciding how much tea to use is left to the consumer
- the measuring of the leaf is a very important part of the traditional tea-brewing ceremony
- the consumer can assess the quality of a tea from the appearance and aroma of the wet leaves as well as from the taste of the liquor

Disadvantages of loose-leaf tea

- if leaf tea is allowed to brew for too long the liquor will become bitter and harsh
- it is necessary to separate the leaves from the water at the end of the correct brewing time by lifting out the infuser basket or by straining the tea liquor from the brewing pot into a second, clean, warm pot in order to prevent the liquor becoming bitter
- perfect brewing needs the correct temperature of water, careful measuring of the leaf and timing of the brew—this vital element in the performance of brewing takes time and concentration
- using leaf tea requires more equipment than tea bags, making it less convenient in the workplace

Interpreting Tea Leaves

Leaves scattered near the handle represent personal and home life. Leaves to the left of the handle represent the past and leaves to the right indicate the future. Those on the opposite side of the cup represent far-off events and people, while those in the bottom are to do with difficult emotions. The area around the rim signifies happy times and positive events and the ring that runs halfway around the inside of the cup is connected with everyday emotions and events.

Best of British

Traditional afternoon tea destinations

Although many tearooms, restaurants and cafes in Britain offer afternoon tea, there are certain iconic places that are famed for their delicate china, vast array of teas, genteel service and elegant surroundings. And if you do head out to afternoon tea, don't plan on eating dinner for a good few hours afterwards, if at all—those dainty little morsels are surprisingly filling!

For afternoon tea in a castle try Amberley Castle in West Sussex.

Iconic destinations

Perhaps one of the most famous purveyors of fine teas is Fortnum & Mason, opposite the Royal Academy of Arts on London's Piccadilly. They have been selling tea for over 300 years, and their new Diamond Jubilee Tea Salon was opened by Her Majesty The Queen in March 2012. Silver service and faultless sandwiches, cakes and pastries are to be expected, and if you feel inspired you can purchase some delicious tea to take home in the department store downstairs.

Hot on the heels of Fortnum & Mason are The Dorchester, The Waldorf and The Ritz, again in London. Iconic hotels with popular afternoon tea menus, booking in advance is a must. Liberty & Co is another iconic London building,

but more famed for its fabrics and fashions than its victuals. However, head to the café and you'll find a delicious afternoon tea menu on offer: perfect refreshment after a day's shopping.

Heading out of the capital to other British cities, you could try tea at The Royal Crescent Hotel in Bath, either in the secret gardens or the cozy lounge complete with roaring fire. A Scottish take on afternoon tea at The Balmoral Hotel on Edinburgh's Princes Street will include a welcome by kilted footmen, or head to Ynyshir Hall in Wales, once owned by Queen Victoria, for a Welsh version. If the Emerald Isle takes your fancy Dublin's Shelbourne Hotel is perfect, with its view of St Patrick's Cathedral and Trinity College.

Country chic
For a more laid-back afternoon tea surrounded by Great British countryside, there are plenty of historic properties with an array of teas on offer. Coworth Park in Berkshire is close to Ascot, home of the Royal horse racing. Holme Lacy House in the Wye Valley is set in magnificent grounds and dates all the way back to 1674. For a touch of Royal glamor head to Sandringham in Norfolk—it's good enough for the Queen!

Further north Farington Lodge in Lancashire is a beautiful Georgian house set in manicured grounds—or head to the Old Swan Hotel in Harrogate, where crime writer Agatha Christie famously disappeared in 1926.

The Dorchester
Park Lane London W.1

Top 5 London Favorites

The Ritz
Glitz and glamor near Green Park

The Waldorf
Traditional treat in Covent Garden

The Dorchester
Pastries and more on Park Lane

Fortnum & Mason
Royal heritage on Piccadilly

Liberty & Co
Tudor style on Regent Street

For a bit of extra historical context take a tour of Blenheim Palace just outside Oxford, and then take tea in the beautiful Indian Room.

Tips
&
Techniques

Successful Baking

Some of the most important keys to successful baking are good quality, appropriate ingredients, correct oven temperature and careful pan preparation. Follow the advice below and you'll be well on your way to creating afternoon tea delights to be proud of.

The right ingredients

Flour

- All-purpose flour is generally used when little rise is required; for example, pastries and shortbreads. To convert all-purpose flour to self-rising flour, add baking powder in the quantities recommended on the container for different types of baking.
- Self-rising flour is used for cakes that need a raising agent. In some recipes, however, the amount of raising agent already added to the flour may be too great; a mixture of all-purpose and self-rising flour is therefore used.
- Always store flour in a cool, dry place, preferably in an airtight container. Sift to remove any lumps and also to incorporate extra air before adding to the cake batter.

Raising agents

- Baking powder is the most commonly used raising agent. It gives off carbon dioxide, which forms bubbles in the batter. These expand during cooking, making the cake, scone or cookie rise and helping to produce a light texture. Too much baking powder can cause heaviness.
- Baking soda is often used in recipes that include sour milk or buttermilk, spices, molasses and honey.
- Sour milk is sometimes used to give extra rise to heavy batters. It can be made by leaving milk in a warm place until it curdles.
- Buttermilk is a standard ingredient in Welsh and Irish cookery.
- Yeast was once the only raising agent available for home baking, but is now generally used only in bread-making and in some traditional fruit or spice breads or

pastries, such as Suffolk Fourses, Chelsea Buns and Lardy Cake. Dried yeast keeps for several months in an airtight container. Fresh yeast lasts for about a week in the refrigerator and will freeze for up to six months. Fresh yeast is often available from large supermarkets with bakeries, or local bakers. You may have to ask for it as it is not a "shelf" item, but it is frequently free of charge. Dried or instant yeast can be substituted for fresh yeast. For ½ oz fresh yeast use ¼ oz dried or instant yeast, for 1 oz fresh yeast use ½ oz dried or instant yeast and for 2 oz fresh yeast use ¾ oz dried or instant yeast. If using dried yeast, dissolve in a little liquid of the recipe before adding to the other ingredients. If using instant yeast, add to the dry ingredients before mixing in the other ingredients. If using dried or instant yeast, the dough only needs to rise once.

Fats

- Butter and margarine are interchangeable in most recipes, but butter is preferable in shortbreads and rich fruit cakes, such as Christmas cake, that are to be stored for some time and matured.
- Shortening, e.g. Crisco is often used in cookies and gives a shorter texture.

- Oil is excellent in carrot cakes and chocolate cakes, and is ideal for anybody with a cholesterol problem.
- Allow butter, margarine or shortening to soften to room temperature for at least an hour before using. Soft or whipped margarines can be used straight from the refrigerator.

Eggs

- Eggs should be at room temperature, as taken straight from the refrigerator they are more likely to curdle.
- Small eggs (sizes 5 and 6) are too small for most recipes. Use large (sizes 1 and 2) or medium (sizes 3 and 4), depending on what the recipe specifies.

Sugar

- Superfine sugar is generally used for creamed batters as it gives a much lighter texture than other types.
- Granulated sugar is acceptable in rubbed-in batters, but can produce a slightly gritty texture. It is worth paying a little extra for superfine sugar.
- Soft brown sugar gives a caramel flavor and beats well in creamed batters. The darker variety has a stronger flavor.
- Demerara sugar is very good in teabreads and in batters where ingredients are melted together,

such as gingerbreads and boiled fruit cakes. It is excellent for sprinkling on the top of loaves and cookies.
- Molasses has a dark color and strong flavor and is often used in gingerbreads and.
- Corn syrup gives a soft, moist, sometimes sticky texture which is suitable for gingerbreads and flapjacks.
- Honey adds a very distinctive flavor but too much will cause the batter to burn easily.

Lining pie dishes and plates

Roll out the pastry to a thickness of about ⅛–¼ in and a little larger in size than the prepared dish or plate. Lay the pastry carefully on the dish, making sure that no air is trapped underneath.
Do not stretch the pastry as it will only shrink back. If it is not big enough, roll out a little more and try again. Ease the pastry into all the rims and corners of the dish, then trim off any surplus.

(Trimmings may be useful to make crosses on hot cross buns or a trellis over the top of a tart or pie.)

Preparing pans

Most non-stick cake pans are very reliable if you follow the manufacturers' instructions but, to be on the safe side, it is wise to line and grease them anyway. Grease pans with whatever fat or oil is to be used in the recipe, then line with non-stick parchment paper. Cut a single piece for the bottom of the pan and, when fitting paper to the sides, cut into the corners to make quite sure that it lies neatly against the pan. It may also be necessary to cut and overlap the paper, as the sides of circular pans sometimes slope slightly.

Oven temperatures

Always make sure that the oven has reached the correct temperature before putting in the item to be baked. If you are not sure whether your oven temperature gauge is accurate, buy an oven thermometer and make regular checks. If you are using a convection (fan-assisted) oven, reduce all recommended temperatures by 68°F.

Is it ready?

To see if a sponge cake is ready, press lightly with a finger; if it springs back, it is cooked. To test fruitcakes and gingerbreads, stick a skewer into the middle of the cake and withdraw it immediately. If the skewer comes out clean, the cake is done. If not, allow a further 15 minutes and test again. Cookies are usually ready when they are just turning golden. Scones are firm, well risen and golden when cooked. If a cake begins to darken too quickly, place a double or triple layer of parchment paper over the top and continue cooking as usual.

Pastry know-how

The aim is to make pastry as light as possible, and this depends on how much cold air is trapped in the dough before baking. The secret is to use cold ingredients, to have cold hands, cold bowls, a cold slab or surface on which to roll (marble is ideal) and to work in a cool room. Work quickly and lightly, using the fingertips when rubbing in, as too much handling makes the pastry tough. When rolling, sprinkle only a little flour on to the work surface and use light, even movements. Most pastry recipes call for all-purpose flour, but self-rising is sometimes used for suet crust and shortcrust. The more fat is used, the shorter the pastry will be; if the amount of fat is less than half the amount of flour, add 1 tsp of baking powder for each 1²/₃ cups of flour. Butter, or butter mixed with shortening, is best. Rich pastry needs a hotter oven than others. If the oven is too cool, the fat will run out of the pastry and the pastry will be tough and chewy.

Baking blind

This is necessary when an uncooked filling is to be put into the pastry case, or to set the pastry before any filling is poured in and cooked. When the prepared pan has been greased and lined with the pastry, prick the base all over with a fork. Cover the base with a piece of parchment paper followed by a layer of baking beans (available in any good cookware store) or pasta or pulses (dried haricot beans, dried kidney beans or chickpeas). Bake in a preheated oven for just under the required time, then remove from the oven, lift out the baking beans and the parchment paper and bake for 5 minutes more to dry out the base.

Crumple your baking parchment and open out again to make it easier to place in your pan.

Top tips

Ovens and their vagaries are always a bit of a nightmare when it comes to writing recipes. Even if we all had the same make and model of oven, I would bet that they would all cook slightly differently. So, bearing in mind that some of us have fan ovens, some have gas, some have Agas, some have snazzy and some have basic, there is no way that if a recipe says "bakes in 20 minutes" you can take that as the law.

In baking there is an element of using your own judgement as well as following a recipe. Have a peep at the cake at least 5 minutes before the end of the allotted time and see whether it's time to a) retrieve it; b) cover it with a bit of greaseproof paper to prevent the top burning and give it another 10 minutes; or c) just to leave it another 5 minutes. It's a judgement call—yours. A cake is generally done when a sharp knife or skewer stuck into it comes back clean without any globs of raw cake batter sticking to it. It should be firm to the touch, and in the case of a sponge, have a bit of a spring to it when you give it a mild poke. Finger sinking into the midst—not good. Being able to rap your knuckles on the top of a carbonated surface—also not good.

So, you've followed all the instructions and something has still gone wrong. Here follows a small compendium of what might have caused the problem and, ultimately, how to wriggle your way out of it.

Never admit that the cake you present with a flourish is not what you had first envisaged. A cake is a wonderful thing, full stop. No one need ever know, and only a very mean-spirited person would comment negatively about a cake that someone else has made. In fact, take the cake away from them—they don't deserve it. They can watch other people eat it. That'll teach them.

Oven tips

Now it may seem obvious, but try to use your common sense when you're baking. Every oven is different and has its own special foibles. Some ovens cook slightly quicker, some slightly slower. Some ovens have "hot patches" so you'll need to turn the sheet to prevent half your cakes or cookies browning more than the other half. So, all ovens cook differently, and I don't want to be responsible for your burnt or raw cakes. Cakes are done if they are firm to the touch and a bit springy on top. You can also insert a toothpick into the center—if it comes out clean, the cake is done.

Muffin tips

I'd like to pretend there's a huge amount of skill and talent involved in baking a batch of golden-brown, sweetly scented muffins—but I'm afraid I'd be lying. They are so unbelievably easy-peasy to make, pretty much anyone can do it—even self-professed failures in the kitchen. But there are a few secrets to making really light fluffy muffins that differ from cakes and cookies—see in particular point three below (which may well appeal directly to the more slapdash cooks among us).

Number 1: To make a sweeping generalization—combine your dry ingredients, combine your wet ingredients, put the two together and bingo: 12 muffins! But before you get to this stage, there's a golden rule...

Number 2: Even if this seems like a pain do it anyway! Sift all your dry ingredients together before you add the wet ingredients. You want your flour, sugar, cocoa, etc. to be as light as air, filling your mixing bowl in soft drifts like freshly fallen snow.

Number 3: Once you add the wet ingredients, don't over-mix! The temptation will be to give the batter a good old beating to make sure you've got a lovely smooth batter. But this is wrong, wrong, wrong. Give it a gentle, brief stir—just enough to combine the ingredients, but no more than that. The average muffin batter will still look a bit lumpy and chunky, and if you've still got a few streaks of flour—don't worry about it. Just scoop up big spoonfuls of the batter, dollop them into the cases, then pop the pan in the oven. Twenty minutes later you'll be in heaven and wondering why you don't make these gorgeous creations every morning.

And if you don't follow this advice? Well, they'll still be edible, but your muffins won't have that fabulously fluffy texture that all the best muffins should have. They'll be a little tough, a little bit more solid than you'd like. So take my advice and always give your muffins the quick 1-2-3 treatment.

Batches of cookies

Now we need to have a full and frank discussion about how many cookies each recipe makes. Most recipe books have a little bit saying "makes 24 cookies" or something similar. Each recipe in this book will make one batch—a do-able, edible batch. You shouldn't have so few as to make it not worthwhile and you shouldn't have too many so you are eating them for weeks. The problem with stating numbers is that I positively want you to use different sorts of cutters. How the devil do you work out how many cookies would be made using a heart-shaped cutter, if someone decides to use a giant T-Rex cutter? If you roll the dough two more times than me, you'll have a thinner cookie and you'll get more. Do you see my point? My small teaspoon is going to be different from your small teaspoon. Embrace the unknown, just make the cookies and enjoy them—don't let yourself get hung up on the fact that a recipe says "makes 24" and you've got 12—or 45.

Melting chocolate

A word here is needed about melting chocolate. There are two methods of melting chocolate (three, if you count giving it to a child to hold in the back of a car). The first is the safest method! Place the chopped-up chocolate in a heatproof bowl over a pan of barely simmering water. The crucial thing here is that the bottom of the bowl must not touch the water; the chocolate gets too hot. Nightmare: grainy ghastly mess; straight into the bin; tears. Don't do it.

The second method is quicker, more gung-ho, and I like to think of it as the rapid assault method of melting chocolate. Quick, brutal— but not without risk: the microwave. Put the chopped chocolate into a microwaveable container, then zap it. Do short bursts of only 10–15 seconds and stir between each zapping. I recommend you stop while there are still some lumps and just keep stirring—the residual heat will melt the rest. The danger here is going for the burn (especially with white chocolate): one second, it is fine and dandy and thoroughly enjoying its little warm-up; the next second, Whoa! All gone horribly, horribly wrong. Have you ever tasted burnt chocolate? Nasty.

Most types of cookie dough freeze well for up to a month if you wrap them carefully in parchment paper and plastic wrap, so if a recipe makes what looks like too much, simply freeze half for another occasion.

Troubleshooting tips

If your cake is solid and brick-like, it might be for a couple of reasons: you may not have beaten enough air into the batter (did you use a wooden spoon and come over all weak?), or if the recipe required you to fold in the flour, you may have been a bit too vigorous and bashed all the air out of your batter.

If your cake is a bit dry and crumbly, the batter might have been too stiff and dry and the oven temperature may have been a little on the high side. Next time, lower the oven temperature and add a splash of milk to the batter.

If the fruit sinks to the bottom of your cake, it's generally because it's too damp or sticky. I always rinse and dry candied cherries. The batter may have been a bit too soft to carry the fruit as it rises.

A cake that's sinking in the middle may be due to a couple of reasons: there may have been too much raising agent, or too soft a batter. Check the oven temperature, too. An oven that is too hot or too cool can cause a cake to sink.

Don't throw out a cake because of its texture. If it is inedible as a cake, make it into cake crumbs and freeze them—there are lots of uses for cake crumbs in other recipes and it's handy to have a stash tucked away. If the cake is flat and tragic, use a cutter to cut out shapes and sandwich them together with jam or buttercream.

With a cake that has risen unevenly, just level the top, turn it upside down and ice the bottom.

A cake with a massively sunken middle can be turned into a mega pudding; cut out the center and pile whipped cream and fruit into the hole. A dusting of confectioners' sugar, and voilà!

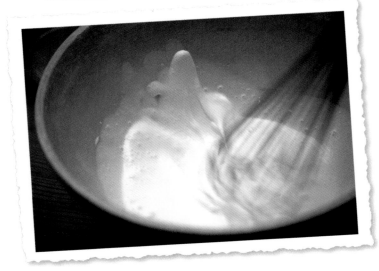

The Frosting on the Cake

Here are three very straightforward types of frosting that you can easily whip up to adorn your baked goodies. The first is glacé frosting made with water or lemon juice. It's a question of sieving the confectioners' sugar, adding the liquid and stirring. That's it. The second frosting is buttercream. Butter, sifted confectioners' sugar. Stir (albeit quickly in a beating-type manner). Flavors, colors and embellishments may be added, but they are a cinch.

Even simpler is spreading something on top a cake or muffin straight out of a jar or tub. Why not? Nutella, lemon curd, mascarpone, whipped heavy cream—all delicious and simply divine spread on top. I feel I should point out that low in effort doesn't actually mean low in cost. An Extremely Posh Rose Cupcake is really quite extravagant—those roses don't come cheap. Hey-ho. All worth it in the world of cupcake exquisiteness!

For cakes that involve a bit more fiddling and twiddling and where you have to make some decorations in advance, rolled fondant frosting is the order of the day. Fondant is made with powdered confectioners' sugar which generally has had some dried glycerine added to it. It's versatile, easy to handle and comes in a wide range of colors.

You will see that I am partial to a drop of color on my cake. I remember one woman wanting reassurance that the electric-blue cake that little Crispin was about to tuck into was entirely natural. I looked at the vivid blue and looked at her and had to break it to her that, in fact, there was nothing very natural about a food item that bright. Having said that, there are companies out there who produce quite a range of tartrazine-free colors for those whose eyes start spinning and their skin forming a thin film of sweat when it comes to artificial colors—and that's just the parents waiting for their children to absorb the color and go on a behaviour free fall. Gels are much better than the liquid colorings. They don't thin the frosting and the colors tend to be much more versatile. I love them. You can get them from good kitchen stores and sugarcraft specialsts. Word of warning: a little goes a long way.

Glacé frosting
Makes enough for 12 cupcakes

This is the simplest and most useful frosting. Minimum ingredients and minimum fuss. Very easily correctible if you make it too thick or too thin.

1¼ cups confectioners' sugar, sifted
Juice of 1 large lemon OR ¼ cup boiling water
Gel food coloring of your choice

1 Put the sifted confectioners' sugar in a bowl. Add the liquid slowly, a little at a time, and stir until smooth. Stop adding liquid when you like the look of the consistency. It should be a smidgen thicker than heavy cream. Add a tiny amount of color—use a cocktail stick/toothpick dipped into the color. You can always add more if you want, but there is no way to undo a lurid amount of color without making a super-huge batch of frosting.

Buttercream
Makes enough for 12 cupcakes

Not for those watching their waistlines, this righ, sweet, melt-in-the-mouth frosting is equally delicious as a filling between layers of cake. Just make sure you beat it really well so it is light and fluffy.

1½ cups confectioners' sugar, sifted
1 stick soft unsalted butter
½ tsp vanilla extract (optional)

1 Beat everything together in a large bowl for a few minutes until light and fluffy. If the mixture looks a little on the heavy side, ½ tsp boiling water whisked in works wonders.

2 If you want colored or flavored buttercream, add away to your heart's content (see suggestions opposite).

Royal icing
Makes enough for 24 cupcakes

This is a great frosting for decorating. It's not that tricky, but you need to watch the consistency. A frosting that hold peaks like a meringue is what you need.

2 large free-range egg whites
About 3¼ cups confectioners' sugar, sifted
2 tsp freshly squeezed lemon juice

1 Put everything into a large mixing bowl, and whisk away for 4–5 minutes until the mixture is very white and standing in stiff peaks. It should be really quite stiff. If the mixture is too cement-like, add a few drops of lemon juice or boiling water. If it is too runny, add a little more sifted confectioners' sugar. This makes a lot of , so you may wish to halve the quantity, but it does keep well for around a week in the refrigerator if you seal it really well. I put a layer of plastic wrap on top of the surface, then seal in an airtight plastic container.

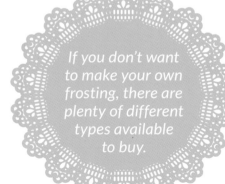

If you don't want to make your own frosting, there are plenty of different types available to buy.

Tasty buttercream

COFFEE
Add 1 tsp very, very, very strong espresso or filter coffee (made with instant coffee—3 tsp coffee granules with just enough boiling water to make it liquid). Mix through thoroughly.

CHOCOLATE
Add 2 tsp sifted cocoa powder to the buttercream mixture. If you want it more chocolatey, add more. If you are feeling very extravagant, melt 2 oz good-quality bittersweet (at least 70% cocoa solids) chocolate in a bowl over a pan of simmering water, and add that, too. Mix through thoroughly.

LEMON
Add the grated zest of 1 unwaxed lemon and 2 tsp freshly squeezed lemon juice. Mix through thoroughly. This works well with lime, too. And orange, come to that.

ROSE
Add a teaspoon of rosewater to the buttercream and mix thoroughly. Taste, and add more rosewater as necessary. Do not confuse rosewater with rose extract: The latter is very powerful and you'll only need one or two tiny drops in your buttercream.

Using a decorating bag

Many people are put off using a decorating bag because it looks a little bit tricky. The key is to practice first on a plate or piece of paper until you get the feel for it and are able to control the flow of frosting from the tube. And once you can do that, you're well on your way to professional-looking cakes, cupcakes and cookies—and you'll be able to use your new-found skills with both buttercream and royal icing.

Decorating tubes

The tubes are the metal or plastic cone-shaped pieces that you place inside the decorating bag. The frosting is squeezed through the tube, and different types of tube give different effects. A small plain round end is best to start with, to practice simple lines and dots with royal icing. Then you can experiment with the different patterns made with different tube ends. For buttercream, use a star-shaped tube at first to practice swirls. These are particularly effective on cupcakes!

You can control the size of your dots by squeezing more or less icing through the tube, and can create patterns just by changing the size of the dots.

Decorating with royal icing

Royal icing is great for adding details to cakes, cookies and cupcakes. It is also very simple to mix with coloring pastes so can be used to add little splashes of color to an otherwise plain treat.

Dots
The consistency of your royal icing is absolutely crucial—too stiff and your dots will be awkward-shaped peaks; too runny and your lines will disappear into the background. Experiment until you get it just right, and only then make a start on your cakes! Hold the bag comfortably in your writing hand, moving it around until you feel in control of the tube. Practice dots first on a plate or piece of card. Hold the decorating bag so the tube is just slightly above and perpendicular to the surface to be decorated. In one smooth movement, squeeze the bag so the pools around the tube, release the pressure on the bag and then pull the tube upwards and away from the dot. The dot should settle to form a perfect dome. If it still has a peak after a couple of minutes, your royal icing is too stiff.

Lines
To create lines, hold the decorating bag in the same way as for dots, but angle the tip at about 45 degrees to the surface you are decorating. Touch the tip of the tube to the surface, then start squeezing the decorating bag at the same time as you start moving the tube slowly across your surface. Ensure you keep the tube moving at the same rate as the flow of royal icing for a smooth line—too fast and you will break the line; too slow and you will get an uneven width. To finish a line neatly touch the tip of the tube to the surface, release the pressure on the bag and bring the tube up and away from the surface, much the same as piping dots.

Decorating with buttercream

Buttercream is so simple to make, and if you go the extra mile and apply it with a decorating bag you'll be rewarded with professional, beautiful results. You can then use sprinkles, sugar decorations, chocolate chips—anything edible and pretty to enhance your buttercream topping. Or you can leave it plain and let the swirls steal the show.

Swirls

Choose a tube that has a star-shaped end, and is reasonably large (about ½ in in diameter). It's great to use a saucer to practice with, as you can use the indented circle in the center. Rest the decorating bag tube at the outside edge of the indented circle (or if using a plate, an imaginary circle around 2½ in in diameter). At the same time, begin steadily squeezing the bag and moving the tube around the outside of the circle. Keep squeezing and moving until you get back to where you started, and continue on the inside of the buttercream circle. You are creating a spiral, which on a flat surface will remain quite flat, but on a domed cupcake will make a wonderful conical shape. Once you reach the center, release the pressure on the decorating bag and pull it vertically upward to finish the swirl with a soft peak.

Ruffles

Buttercream ruffles are particularly good around the vertical sides of a tall cake, or around the outer edge of the top of a gateau. Choose a tube that has a long and narrow opening, either with or without a crimped edge. Practice first on a plate or piece of card. Place the end of the tube at about 45 degrees to the surface, long side down. Squeeze the decorating bag and gently but surely move it half an inch back, quarter inch forward, half an inch back, quarter inch forward and so on to create a ruffled effect.

Try twisting the tube and bag slightly as you work for an even swirlier swirl!

When decorating with buttercream try to keep your hands cool so it doesn't start to melt in the bag. Keep turning the bag, and put it in the refrigerator for 15 minutes if it begins to feel too warm and soft.

Knead it!

Nothing compares to the scent of homemade bread baking in the oven. Morning, noon or night, it'll cheer up your home and induce healthy appetites for everyone within its walls!

The most commonly used type of flour for breadmaking is wheat flour. Wheat bread flour has a high gluten content and gives a better volume of bread, as it absorbs more water and makes a lighter dough.

White flour is made from the starchy part of the grain from which the fiber and wheatgerm has been removed. Whole-wheat flour is made from 100 percent of the grain; nothing is added and nothing is taken away. Wheatmeal is made from 81–85 percent of the grain and some of the fiber and wheatgerm has been removed.

Bread can be made with various other grains. Rye gives a dark dough and is usually mixed half and half with wheat flour; barley gives a cake-like texture and is usually mixed with wheat flour; maize gives a crumbly, crunchy texture. Other ingredients can be added to achieve different results: for example, extra bran, wheatgerm, sesame, poppy or sunflower seeds, cheese, herbs, spices, lemon or orange rind and rye flakes.

Kneading

Kneading is an essential part of breadmaking as it helps to develop the gluten and the rise of the dough. Flour a board and use the palms of the hands, almost to the wrists, to push and turn the dough. As you work you can actually feel the texture changing to a smooth, elastic but not sticky consistency. Don't underestimate the amount of time and energy that's needed to turn your dough from initial mix to perfectly smooth and elastic bread dough. It's a fantastic work out for your arms, so get some music on and pump those fists! Had a hard day at work? Kids driving you nuts? Breadmaking is particularly good therapy for getting rid of all those frustrations.

Fresh or dried yeast?

Dried or instant yeast can be substituted for fresh yeast. For ½ oz fresh yeast use ¼ oz/ dried or instant yeast, for 1 oz fresh yeast use ½ oz dried or instant yeast and for 2 oz fresh yeast use ¾ oz dried or instant yeast. If using dried yeast, dissolve in a little liquid of the recipe before adding to the other ingredients. If using instant yeast, add to the dry ingredients before mixing in the other ingredients. If using dried or instant yeast, the dough only needs to rise once.

Always check the use by date on your yeast—dried yeast doesn't keep for as long as you might think and if it's out of date your bread won't rise!

Rising

Always cover the dough when setting it to rise; any drafts may affect the rising process, and even without drafts you don't want the surface of your dough to dry out. The yeast in the dough needs warmth to start working; the ideal temperature is 98–110°F. Too much heat will kill the yeast; too little will prevent it from working. The time taken for the dough to rise will depend on the surrounding warmth, but it usually takes 1–1½ hours. The second rising is much quicker, usually between 20 minutes and half an hour.

Troubleshooting

If the loaf is smaller than expected, the yeast probably did not activate properly due to incorrect temperature during rising. If the texture is coarse, the yeast was not properly mixed at the beginning, or there was too much yeast, which caused excessive rising and air in the dough.

Many freestanding mixers come with a dough hook. This can save you a lot of toil—just follow the manufacturer's instructions for the best results.

Flour Power

The flour we are all familiar with is milled from wheat grains—but it can be made from all kinds of different starchy grains, which is good news for those of us intolerant of wheat and gluten.

Chestnut flour
Chestnut flour has a natural sweetness and nutty flavor. It works particularly well in dense, chocolatey cakes. It's available from larger supermarkets and specialst food stores, and online.

Gram/chickpea flour
Use this sparingly, as it can leave a slightly bitter aftertaste. However, it's great blended with other flours in savory pastries. Readily available online and from Asian food stores.

Coconut flour
Coconut flour has a dominant flavor, which works well where you want a coconut flavor, but it's not generally interchangeable with other flours.

Cornstarch
Cornstarch is great in shortbreads as it lends a "melt-in-the- mouth" quality. Best used blended with other flours, as it hasn't enough body to be used on its own.

Linseed/Flaxseed (brown, ground)
The nutty, sweet flavor and high moisture content of this flour makes it a really delicious ingredient. It is often interchangeable with sorghum, millet and gluten-free oat flours. It is available from wholefood stores and from some supermarket "free from" ranges, or online.

Hazelnut flour
Hazelnut meal flour is available online. Alternatively, you can toast and grind your own nuts.

Millet flour
Allergycare millet flour is available from various online suppliers.

Oats and oat flour
Strictly gluten-free oats and gluten-free oat flour can be difficult to source due to possible contamination from wheat or other cereals in the field or mill—and some celiacs are sensitive even to pure oats. Millet flour and millet flakes are a good alternative if you'd prefer to avoid oats.

Polenta
For baking, use dry, finely ground cornmeal (not the pre-cooked polenta blocks). It's great mixed with other flours or ground nuts.

Quinoa flour
Quinoa isn't technically a grain, but a seed, and is incredibly nutritious. The flour is available online and in some wholefood stores.

Rice flour
Brown rice flour is available online and in some wholefood stores and supermarkets. Glutinous rice flour is also gluten-free: "glutinous" refers to the stickiness of the rice. Available from Asian food stores and online.

Sorghum flour/juwar
This fabulous flour produces a lovely fluffy cake texture and can be used blended or on its own. Available from Asian food stores, or online.

Cassava/tapioca flour
Tapioca flour is similar to cornstarch: it's very soft and neutral in flavor. Best used blended with other flours. It is available in wholefood stores and online.

Gluten-free baking

Gluten-free cooking can be exciting and creative, and the results utterly gorgeous. Just like any other cooking, in fact. Some of the ingredients may sound strange at first, but once you get to know them you'll be able to run with them. It's best to focus on what can be done—brilliantly and deliciously—with the resources available. Don't worry about being able to "translate" traditional recipes to gluten free precisely, as down this path disappointment and vexation lie.

Gluten-free ingredients
Inspiration from Northern Italy includes polenta, and toasted and ground nuts such as almonds, pistachios and hazelnuts, where these ingredients are commonly used. Ground nuts have a softer texture and higher moisture content than rice flours and typical gluten-free flour mixes. Rice flour is a useful ingredient, but only in combination with other flours.

For cakes that will last longer than just a day or two, the natural oiliness of ground nuts helps keep them moist. Ground linseed/flax seed is less expensive than many nuts, however, and can be used to replace some or all of the nuts in a recipe. Linseed has a naturally nutty flavor and a sweetness, and behaves in much the same way as ground almonds in cooking. Sorghum flour and tapioca flour are soft and absorbent, resulting in light, fluffy cakes. Steer clear of potato-derived flours as they can be heavy, and use gram flour/chickpea flour sparingly as it can have a slightly sour taste. Gluten-free oats and oat flour are great for adding texture, but check that they are certified gluten-free, as this is not always the case.

Tips and techniques
Gluten lends stretch and "glue" to a batter or dough. In certain cake recipes, the lack of gluten is not so critical. For example, you can achieve a wonderfully textured brownie using ground almonds in place of wheat flour. Pastry, however, is more of a challenge to create without gluten. When making cakes, brownies and other beaten batters, ensure your ingredients are at room temperature and not straight from the refrigerator. If you add anything too hot or too cold it can cause the batter or dough to shrink during cooking.

If your batter or dough includes beaten eggs, be careful not to pour warm melted butter or chocolate directly onto the eggs, as the heat may cause them to scramble. If baking powder comes into contact with anything acidic, it may react and cause the batter or dough to separate, so it's a good idea to keep it insulated from acidic ingredients such as lemon or orange juice, zest or oil, rhubarb or other acidic fruit. When adding ingredients to a mixing bowl, always try to "sandwich" the baking powder between other dry ingredients.

Pastry
Pastry dough without gluten requires a little TLC. All pastries are easier to handle if chilled in the refrigerator for an hour or so before rolling out. Using a liberal dusting of tapioca flour and rolling pastry mixes between sheets of silicone paper are nifty tricks. With butter-based pastries and crusts you need to work with chilled and cubed or grated butter.

In warmer weather you'll often end up with a stickier dough and in colder weather you may need to mix it for longer and hand-mold it into something workable. You just need the confidence to manually handle it and swiftly squidge it into shape. Sometimes you may need to add a little milk or egg yolk as a binder. Pastry is more vulnerable to variables than other forms of baking: room temperature, moisture levels and your body temperature all have an effect. Sometimes the recipe will specify that you to bake the pastry blind; this works very well in gluten-free pastry and you don't need to line the pastry with baking beans or parchment paper.

Tea Party Ideas & Themes

Hosting your own *Tea Party*

Who could resist an invitation to afternoon tea? Cakes, teabreads, bite-size treats plus plenty of hot tea makes for a delicious party, and you could always ask guests to bring along a sweet treat to share if you don't have time to do all of the catering yourself.

Inviting your guests

We're all so used to texting and emailing to communicate with our friends, the written invitation is becoming a rarity left for weddings. If time allows, invest in some smart notecards and hand-write your invitations—it'll set the mood for your party and delight your guests before they've even arrived.

Vintage fashion has really come to the fore recently, so if you think your guests will be game you could suggest a vintage theme. '50s rockabilly is great fun or break out the flapper dresses and long necklaces for a '20s twist. And let's not forget the royal connections—tiaras and crowns are fun to wear and don't have to contain real gemstones!

Getting ready

As with any party, getting organized is crucial. Make a list of what you need to buy a few days before your tea party, and anything that can be made in advance of party day should be prepared the day or two before if possible. Many teabreads and fruit cakes can be made a few days before and stored in an airtight container.

If you are expecting more than a handful of guests it might be worth having some store-bought stand-by food in case they are all super hungry and gobble up your tea party offerings before the end of the party. It's also a good idea to find out about dietary requirements too. You could always make little flags on cocktail sticks to label different dishes if you have allergy sufferers in attendance.

A vintage theme adds a quirky edge to any tea party

A pretty tea dress or casual suit are the perfect attire for afternoon tea—and as the host or hostess you could don a retro apron in case of spills!

Lovely linens

A proper tea party is a fabulous excuse to dig out your grandmother's linens from the closet, wash and press them if need be, and let them be useful once more. Or if you don't have any tablecloths and cloth napkins in the house, now could be the time to either borrow from your family or make an investment and treat yourself to your very own.

Best china

If you have (or can borrow) some traditional teacups and saucers then do so—it'll add proper elegance to your party. Make sure you clean and polish all the china ahead of the day, and don't use any cups with cracks or chips. And don't worry of your teacups don't match—an assortment of styles and patterns not only looks great but will help guests to know which one is theirs!

Spick and span

For any elegant party such as afternoon tea, it's important to create the right environment for your guests. Make sure your surfaces sparkle and clear away any clutter either to rooms the guests won't be in or into cupboards. And if all that's too much to do on top of preparing delicious treats, then get some help!

Tea Party Menus

These clever ideas are perfect for hosting your own Tea Party. Simply choose your theme and get baking. Now all you need is the Mad Hatter...

Vintage Tea Party Menu

Selection of Smoked
Salmon Sandwiches

❧

Sliced Earl Grey Loaf . . . **139**

❧

Chelsea Buns . . . **130**

❧

Light Sponge Cake . . . **64**

❧

Served with a Selection of Organic
Fair-Trade Loose Leaf Teas

Wow your friends and family with this oh-so-British menu

You'll be voted Best Mom with this creative fare

Little Ones' Tea Party Menu

Selection of cheese sandwiches

Fondant Fancies . . . **178**

Chocolate Orange Drizzle Cake . . . **78**

Fruit Scones . . . **118**

Served with Home-Made Lemonade

Party Menus

Get the girls round for a relaxing evening and treat everyone to some delicious
home-baked goodies, and remember that birthday fun isn't just for kids.
Get those candles out and make sure everyone sings!

Girls' Night In

Smoked Salmon Muffins . . . **210**

Upside Down Polenta Plum Cake . . . **228**

Soft Berry Cookies . . . **236**

Macarons . . . **148**

*Don't forget
to chill some drinks
and send the boys
out for the evening
before they eat all
the cakes!*

Sweet treats aren't for everyone— but you could always include one of the savory muffin recipes on pages 204–212 as well.

Grown-up Birthday Party

Summer party Menus

Have fun in the sun with these delicious party menus—whether you need baked treats that are easy to pack up and take on a picnic, or are entertaining at home in the summer.

Perfect Picnic

Cheddar & Rosemary Bread . . . **214**

Banbury Cakes . . . **94**

Carrot Cupcakes . . . **160**

Apricot Sesame
Slice . . . **108**

Be realistic about what you can carry. Disposable plates, cutlery and cups will lighten the load and can then be thrown away.

Elegant Garden Party

Kids' Party Menus

Kids love parties but planning a fun-filled event AND delicious treats can be a headache. The key is in the preparation … and having a few clever tricks up your sleeve.

Boys' Party Menu

Chocolate Cake . . . **70**

Peppermint Stick
Muffins . . . **158**

Boys' Own Cupcakes . . . **196**

Colored Candies . . . **200**

Fresh Orange & Apple Juice

Mini packs of raisins make brilliant snacks and tasty party bag fillers.

Girls' Party Menu

Dazzle your little guests with these sweet treats!

Birthday Mini Muffins . . . **201**

Rocky Roadsters . . . **190**

Custard Creams . . . **230**

Jam Doughnuts . . . **174**

Homemade Lemonade

The
Basics

Classic Cake Recipes

Madeira cake
Makes 1 x 7 in round cake

1⅔ cups all-purpose flour, sifted
1 tsp baking powder
1½ sticks butter, softened
¾ cup superfine sugar
Grated rind of ½ lemon
3 eggs
2 tbsp milk

1 Preheat the oven to 350°F. Grease and line a 7 in round cake pan. Mix together the flour and baking powder. Beat together the butter, sugar and lemon rind until light and fluffy. Beat in the eggs, one at a time, adding 2 tbsp of flour with the last two. Fold in the remaining flour, then gently mix in the milk.

2 Turn into the prepared pan and bake for 1 hour until a skewer comes out clean. Remove from the oven and turn out onto a wire rack to cool.

Lemon drizzle cake
Makes 1 x 1 lb loaf

¼ cup soft margarine
Scant ⅔ cup self-rising flour, sifted
Generous ⅓ cup superfine sugar
1 large free-range eggs
2 tbsp milk
Grated zest and juice of 1 unwaxed lemon
½ cup granulated sugar

Try using other flavors with the lemon drizzle recipe: any citrus fruit works well.

1 Preheat the oven to 325°F. Grease and line a 1 lb loaf pan.

2 Put the margarine, flour, superfine sugar, eggs, milk and lemon zest into a large bowl or freestanding mixer and beat until the batter is very pale and fluffy. Spoon the batter into the pan and smooth the surface. Bake for about 30 minutes, or until the cake is firm and springy to the touch and a knife or skewer comes out clean.

3 Mix the lemon juice and granulated sugar in a bowl and as soon as the cake comes out of the oven, spread this mixture over the surface. Leave the cake to cool in its pan and soak up the tangy lemon topping. Turn it out of the pan when it is completely cold.

Whisked sponge cake
Serves 8

3 large free-range eggs, separated
½ cup superfine sugar
Generous ½ cup plus 1 tbsp self-rising flour
⅔ cup heavy cream
Handful of very ripe soft fruit such as blackcurrants, strawberries, raspberries, or redcurrants
Confectioners' sugar for dusting

1 Preheat the oven to 325°F. Grease and line two 8 in layer cake pans.

2 Put the egg yolks and superfine sugar in a bowl and whisk until you have a very thick, pale and fluffy mixture. In another, very clean bowl, whisk the egg whites until they are stiff. Fold the egg whites into the egg yolk mixture. Then sift the flour over the mixture and, with a very light touch, fold the flour in. Divide the dough between the two pans and bake for about 20 minutes or until firm to the touch. Turn the cakes out onto a wire rack to cool.

3 Whip the cream until it's softly thick—don't overbeat it. When the cakes are cold, spread the cream over one of the cakes, scatter the fruit over the cream and top with the second cake.

4 Dust the top with a smattering of confectioners' sugar. This cake is best eaten on the day it is made as it hasn't got any fat in the sponge so will dry out quickly.

Chocolate sandwich cake
Serves 8

1 cup self-rising flour, sifted
¾ cup superfine sugar
¾ cup soft margarine
3 large free-range eggs
1 tbsp milk
Scant ½ cup cocoa powder, sifted
1 stick unsalted butter
1¾ cups confectioners' sugar, sifted
1–2 tsp milk (optional)

1 Preheat the oven to 325°F. Grease and line two 8 in round layer cake pans. In a mixer (preferably), beat together the flour, superfine sugar, margarine, eggs, milk and half the cocoa powder. Beat for about 2 minutes until the batter is pale brown and fluffy. Divide between the two pans and smooth the surfaces. Bake for about 20 minutes or until the tops of the cakes are firm and springy to the touch. Turn out the cakes onto wire racks to cool.

2 While the cakes are cooling, make the buttercream. Beat together the butter, confectioners' sugar and remaining cocoa until soft and fluffy. If necessary, add a teaspoon or so of milk to get a softer consistency—you need to be able to spread this.

3 When the cakes are cold, sandwich them together with half the buttercream and spread the remaining buttercream on the top of the cake.

Cookie and Cupcake Recipes

Simple cupcakes
Makes about 12

Generous ¾ cup self-rising flour, sifted
½ cup superfine sugar, sifted
½ cup margarine, softened
1 tsp baking powder
2 large free-range eggs
1 tsp pure vanilla extract

1 Preheat the oven to 325°F. Line a 12-hole muffin pan with baking cups.

2 Put all the ingredients into a mixer (food processor, food mixer, or just a big bowl with an electric whisk). Mix really well until the batter is light and fluffy.

3 Put heaped teaspoons of the batter into the prepared cups, and bake in the oven for about 20 minutes until golden, and firm and springy to the touch. Let them cool before adding a frosting of your choice to the top.

Basic butter cookies
Makes 1 batch

2¼ sticks butter, softened
1¼ cups confectioners' sugar, sifted
1 tsp vanilla extract
1 large free-range egg yolk
2⅔ cups all-purpose flour

1 Beat the butter and sugar together in a large bowl until very pale and fluffy. Add the vanilla and egg yolk and mix well. Sift in the flour and mix until it forms a firm dough. You may need to get your hands in here and work it into a smooth ball. Wrap the dough in plastic wrap and put it in the refrigerator for an hour. You can freeze it at this stage if you wish.

2 Preheat the oven to 375°F and line two baking sheets with a silicone liner.

3 Roll out the dough on a lightly floured surface until it is about ⅛ in thick, then cut out the shapes you require and place on the lined baking sheets. Bake for 10–12 minutes or until the cookies are pale golden. Transfer the cookies to a wire rack where they will harden as they cool.

Try adding choc chips or dried fruit pieces to simple shortbread.

Chocolate brownies
Makes about 18

1 stick unsalted butter
1¾ oz bittersweet chocolate (at least 70% cocoa solids)
2 large free-range eggs, lightly beaten
1 cup superfine sugar
Generous ⅔ cup all-purpose flour, sifted
1 cup chopped walnuts

1 Preheat the oven to 350°F. Grease and line a 7 x 11 in pan.

2 Pop a heatproof bowl over a pan of barely simmering water, but don't let the bottom of the bowl touch the water. Melt the butter and chocolate in the bowl. Take the pan off the heat and let the mixture cool for about 5 minutes, then tip it into a bigger bowl, add all the other ingredients and give it a good old beat with a wooden spoon.

3 Pour the batter into the prepared pan and level the surface. Bake for about 30 minutes. The top will have crisped over but the middle will still be soggy—don't be afraid to take it out of the oven as it continues to set as it cools. There's nothing worse than an overcooked brownie; you want a decent squidge. Leave it to cool in the pan before cutting it into squares or oblongs.

Simple shortbread
Makes 1 batch

2¼ sticks butter, softened
¼ cup superfine sugar
Scant 2 cups all-purpose flour
Scant 1 cup cornstarch

1 Preheat the oven to 325°F. Cream the butter and sugar together in a large bowl until pale and fluffy. Sift the flour and cornstarch onto the butter mixture and mix until you have a lovely smooth dough. At this stage you can either press it into a square pan, which you have lightly greased, and bake straight away or form it into a fat sausage and wrap it in plastic wrap. Make the sausage as fat as you want the cookies to be round and chill the dough in the refrigerator for at least an hour.

2 Unwrap the dough and slice into circles about ¼ in thick. Place the circles on a silicone-lined baking sheet and bake for about 30–40 minutes until pale and golden. Transfer the shortbread to a wire rack to cool.

3 If you are using a pan, cut the shortbread in the pan while it is still warm and leave to cool in the pan.

Pastry Recipes

Flaky pastry

3¼ cups all-purpose flour, sifted
1 tsp salt
3 sticks butter, or half butter, half
shortening, e.g. Crisco, softened
1 tsp lemon juice
1¼ cups cold water

1 Mix together the flour and salt. Divide the fat into four portions. Rub one portion into the flour with your fingertips. Mix in the lemon juice and cold water to give a soft dough, and knead gently on a lightly floured board until smooth.

2 Roll out the dough to a rectangle three times longer than it is wide. Dot the second portion of fat over the top two-thirds of the surface. Fold up the bottom third and fold down the top third and seal the edges. Wrap in plastic wrap or a plastic bag and chill for 15 minutes.

3 Place the dough on the floured board with the folded edges to your right and left, and roll out again to a rectangle. Repeat the dotting, folding and chilling process twice more until all the fat is used. Wrap again and chill for at least 45 minutes before using.

Puff pastry

3¼ cups all-purpose flour, sifted
1 tsp salt
4 sticks butter, softened
1 tsp lemon juice
About ½ cup iced water

1 Mix together the flour and salt. Add ¼ stick of the butter, cut into small pieces, and rub into the flour until the mixture resembles fine breadcrumbs. Add the lemon juice and enough water to give a soft dough. Knead lightly until really smooth.

2 In a clean linen cloth, shape the remaining butter into a rectangle. On a lightly floured board, roll out the pastry to a rectangle slightly wider than the rectangle of butter and about twice its length.

3 Place the butter on one half of the pastry and fold the other half over. Press the edges together with a rolling pin. Leave in a cool place for 15 minutes to allow the butter to harden slightly.

4 Roll out the pastry to a long strip three times its original length, but keeping the width the same. The corners should be square, the sides straight and the thickness even. The butter must not break through the dough. Fold the bottom third up and the top third down, press the edges together with a rolling pin, put inside a well-oiled plastic bag and chill for 30 minutes.

5 Place the dough on the floured board with the folded edges to your right and left, and roll out into a long strip as before. Fold again into three and chill for a further 30 minutes. Repeat this process four times more and chill for 30 minutes before using.

Remember to keep everything cold when making pastry, even your hands!

Rich shortcrust pastry

3¼ cups all-purpose flour, sifted
A good pinch of salt
3 sticks butter, softened
2 egg yolks
4 tsp superfine sugar
3–4 tbsp cold water

1 Mix together the flour and salt. Rub in the butter until the mixture resembles breadcrumbs. Make a well in the middle, add the egg yolks and sugar and mix with a round-bladed knife. Add enough of the water, a little at a time, to give a stiff but pliable dough. Knead lightly until smooth.

2 Wrap in plastic wrap or a plastic bag and chill in the refrigerator for at least 15 minutes before using.

Rough puff pastry

3¼ cups all-purpose flour, sifted
A pinch of salt
3 sticks butter, softened
1 tsp lemon juice
3–4 tbsp cold water

1 Mix together the flour and salt. Cut the butter into small pieces and stir lightly into the flour with a round-bladed knife. Make a well in the middle, add the lemon juice and mix with enough water to give an elastic dough.

2 On a lightly floured board, roll out the dough to a long strip, keeping the sides straight and the corners square. Fold up the bottom third and fold down the top third and turn the dough so that the folded edges are to your right and left.

3 Repeat the rolling and folding process three times more, chilling the pastry for 15 minutes between the third and fourth rolling. Chill for at least 15 minutes before using.

Shortcrust pastry

3¼ cups all-purpose flour, sifted
A pinch of salt
1 stick butter, softened
½ cup shortening, e.g. Crisco, softened
3–4 tbsp cold water

1 Mix together the flour and salt. Cut the fats into small pieces and rub into the flour until the mixture resembles breadcrumbs.

2 Gradually add enough water, mixing with a fork, to give a stiff, but pliabale dough. Knead lightly until smooth. Wrap in plastic wrap or a plastic bag and chill for at least 15 minutes before using.

It's really important to chill pastry dough before using—don't be tempted to skip this step.

Classic
Cakes

Victoria Sponge

Makes 1 8 in round cake

Aaah. The mother of all everyday cakes. It is like the comforting, delicious faithful friend of the cake world. The house smells gorgeous when it's in the oven, it's a cinch to make and you can vary it by changing the jam in the middle, adding buttercream, fresh cream, luscious strawberries or raspberries when they are at their best—the possibilities are endless. Victoria sponge, we salute you.

1¼ cups self-rising flour, sifted
¾ cup superfine sugar
¾ cup soft margarine
3 large free-range eggs
1 tsp vanilla extract
1 tbsp strawberry jam
Confectioners' sugar for dusting

1   Preheat the oven to 325°F. Grease and line two 8 in round layer cake pans. Put all the ingredients except the jam and the confectioners' sugar in a large bowl and beat the living daylights out of them. The preferred method is in a freestanding mixer, but you could use an electric hand whisk.

2   When the batter is very pale, fluffy and almost mousse-like, divide it between the prepared pans and smooth out. Bake for about 20 minutes. The cakes should be springy to the touch and a skewer or sharp knife should come out clean when poked into the sponge.

3   Cool the cakes on a wire rack. When they are cold, sandwich them together with the jam, and dust the top with confectioners' sugar. Voilà!

Light Sponge Cake

Makes 1
8 in
round
cake

This is a recipe from Chirk Castle in Wales where afternoon tea was a very elegant but small meal consisting of sandwiches the size of a postage stamp. Sometimes in cold weather a dish of hot buttered muffins or warm scones were also served. One footman who used to be responsible for taking tea into the salon once said, "When clearing away the teas I always remember you had to eat at least four sandwiches to even taste them!'

Scant 1 cup granulated or superfine sugar
2 large or 3 medium eggs
1 cup self-rising flour, sifted
A pinch of salt
1 tsp baking powder
½ cup milk
½ stick butter
2–3 drops vanilla essence

1 Preheat the oven to 325°F. Grease and line an 8 in round pan.

2 Beat together the sugar and eggs until thick and creamy. Add the flour, salt and baking powder and mix well.

3 Put the milk in a small pan and heat gently. Melt the butter in the milk and bring to a boil. When boiling, add to the flour mixture with the vanilla essence and beat well to give a runny consistency.

4 Turn into the prepared pan and bang the pan sharply on the table to remove air bubbles. Bake for 20–25 minutes until a skewer comes out clean.

5 Remove from the oven and cool in the pan for 15 minutes before turning out onto a wire rack to cool. completely.

This cake is quick and easy to make, and is delicious served with fruit and cream. It is ideal for freezing.

Everyday Coffee Cake

Makes 1 8 in round cake

I love coffee cake. So scrumptious. The key is to add enough coffee. If you're going to have coffee cake, it really should taste of coffee, don't you think? The walnuts on top are optional—as is the frosting. You could increase the amount of buttercream and put that on top of the cake, if you wish. Alternatively, leave it naked.

1¼ cups self-rising flour, sifted
¾ cup superfine sugar
¾ cup soft margarine
3 large free-range eggs
8 heaped tsp instant coffee granules
3 tsp boiling water
Scant ¾ stick plus 1 tbsp unsalted butter
2½ cups confectioners' sugar, sifted
8 walnut halves

1   Preheat the oven to 325°F. Grease and line two 8 in round layer cake pans. In a mixer, beat together the flour, superfine sugar, margarine and eggs until they are very pale and fluffy.

2   Put the coffee granules in a cup or small bowl and add about 3 tsp boiling water. The coffee should be very, very dark and just runny—if it's a bit stiff, add a few drops more water, but it certainly shouldn't look like ordinary coffee. You want a liquor that will give a huge hit of coffee without having to add too much volume of liquid.

3   Add 1 tsp coffee mixture to the cake mix and beat it in. Taste, and add more coffee if needed. Don't throw away any remaining mixture!

4   Divide the batter between the two pans and smooth out. Bake for about 20 minutes until the cakes are firm and springy to the touch. Cool the cakes on a wire rack while you crack on with the filling and frosting.

5   Beat the butter and 1 cup plus 2 tbsp confectioners' sugar together until pale and soft. Add 1 tsp coffee mixture and taste. If the balance is fine, leave it there, but you may wish to add a little more.

6   In another bowl, add the remaining coffee mixture to the remaining confectioners' sugar and mix until you have a smooth mixture with the consistency of custard. If it's too runny, add more confectioners' sugar; if too thick, add a drop of water.

7   When the sponges are cold, sandwich them together with the buttercream and then frost the top of the cake with the coffee frosting. Place the walnuts around the edge of the cake and leave the frosting to set, which should only take about an hour or so.

Perfect for lovers of marzipan, Simnel cake has a secret layer of it within the cake as well as the top decoration.

Simnel Cake

This traditional cake is made at Easter, the eleven balls of marzipan on the top of the cake symbolizing the twelve apostles minus Judas.

1 lb 4 oz marzipan
1½ sticks butter, softened
¾ cup light soft brown sugar
3 eggs, beaten
½ oz glycerine
½ oz glucose
¾ cup white bread flour
Scant ½ cup all-purpose flour
Scant ⅓ cup ground almonds
1 tsp mixed spice
½ tsp grated nutmeg
2 cups golden raisins
1¾ cups currants
¾ cup mixed candied peel
A little apricot jam for fixing the marzipan topping in place

1   Preheat the oven to 350°F. Grease an 8 in round pan, line with a double layer of parchment paper and grease well.

2   Divide the marzipan into three portions, one slightly smaller than the other two. Set the smallest portion aside and, on a sugared board, roll out one of the two equal portions to a circle just smaller than the diameter of the pan.

3   Beat together the butter and sugar until light and fluffy. Add the beaten eggs, glycerine and glucose and beat again. Mix together the flours, almonds and spices and gradually add to the mixture, stirring gently to blend. Do not beat. Add the dried fruit and fold gently in.

4   Turn half the batter into the prepared pan and smooth the top. Place the circle of marzipan on top and then cover with the remaining cake batter. Smooth the top and bake for 1 hour (if the top starts to become too brown, cover with a double layer of parchment paper), then reduce the oven temperature to 325°F and bake for a further 45 minutes to 1 hour until a skewer comes out clean.

5   Remove from the oven and leave to cool in the pan for about 15 minutes before turning out onto a wire rack to cool completely.

6   When the cake is completely cold, brush the top with apricot jam. Roll out the second portion of marzipan to make a circle to fit the top of the cake. Put it in place and press gently to make sure it is firmly fixed. Form the remaining marzipan into eleven small balls and arrange them around the rim of the cake, sticking them on with a little apricot jam. Turn the broiler to a moderate heat and place the cake underneath for a few minutes until the marzipan just begins to turn a golden brown.

7   To serve, wrap a wide yellow satin ribbon around the cake and fix with a pin. Arrange a small posy of fresh spring flowers on the top.

Basic Chocolate Cake

OK, calling a chocolate cake "basic" might be a bit off-putting, but this is a no-nonsense chocolate sponge sandwich. It is what it is. There's no getting away from it, but it's a cake that is ultimately very yummy and very few people will turn their noses up at the offer of a slice. The crucial thing that makes this cake great rather than OK is the quality of the cocoa you use. Do not, under any circumstances, use drinking chocolate.

1 cup self-rising flour, sifted
¾ cup superfine sugar
¾ cup soft margarine
3 large free-range eggs
1 tbsp milk
Scant ½ cup cocoa powder, sifted
Scant 1 stick unsalted butter
1¾ cups confectioners' sugar, sifted
1–2 tsp milk (optional)
Chocolate callets to decorate (optional)

1   Preheat the oven to 325°F. Grease and line two 8 in round layer cake pans. In a mixer (preferably), beat together the flour, superfine sugar, margarine, eggs, milk and half the cocoa powder. Beat for about 2 minutes until the batter is pale brown and fluffy. Divide between the two pans and smooth the surfaces. Bake for about 20 minutes or until the tops of the cakes are firm and springy to the touch. Turn out the cakes onto wire racks to cool.

2   While the cakes are cooling, make the buttercream. Beat together the butter, confectioners' sugar and remaining cocoa until soft and fluffy. If necessary, add 1 tsp or so of milk to get a softer consistency—you need to be able to spread this.

3   When the cakes are cold, sandwich them together with half the buttercream and spread the remaining buttercream on the top of the cake. Decorate, if you wish, with chocolate callets or any other chocolate that takes your fancy.

Easy Fruit Cake

I am a bit wary of fruit cakes. The term covers those dark, dry numbers with a bit of marzipan and rock-hard frosting that lie in sad little fingers on a tray, getting drier and drier and sadder and sadder. A bad fruit cake is a depressing, soul-destroying affair. A good fruit cake is a wonderful, life-affirming experience that makes you savor the juiciness and richness—and that's even without the addition of a little alcohol. This is a recipe for a boiled fruit cake—the stuff of everyday.

$^2/_3$ cup raisins
$^2/_3$ cup ready-to-eat dried apricots
$^1/_3$ cup dried cherries
$^2/_3$ cup dried peaches (or pears)
$^2/_3$ cup water
1 stick unsalted butter
$^2/_3$ cup dark brown sugar
2 large free-range eggs, beaten
1 tsp mixed spice
$1^2/_3$ cups self-rising flour, sifted

1 Preheat the oven to 300°F. Grease and line an 8 in cake pan. Put the dried fruit, water, butter and sugar into a pan and heat gently until the mixture comes up to simmering point. Simmer for about 20 minutes, giving it a stir every now and again to stop the mixture sticking.

2 Let the mixture cool for a while— if you add the eggs while it's too hot you get scrambled eggs. When it's cool, add the eggs and spice and sift the flour over the top of it all. Mix it all up well—and this is where you really don't need a mixer; a wooden spoon is perfect.

3 Tip the batter into the pan and smooth the top. I like to make a little indent in the center of the cake as I think it helps to prevent it doming. Bake for about 1½ hours, checking after an hour to see if it's done by sticking a knife or a skewer in to see if it comes out clean. If it needs longer in the oven and the top is getting a bit too brown, cover it in parchment paper.

4 Leave the cake to cool in the pan for about 20 minutes before turning out onto a wire rack to cool.

Carrot Cake with Lime Topping

Makes 1 2 lb loaf or 7 in round cake

This is another indulgent cake that should be eaten with little pastry forks. These small, three-pronged tea forks were developed from Victorian dessert forks in the second half of the 19th century. So that a little pressure could safely be exerted on a fruit tartlet or slice of Madeira cake, the first two narrow prongs of the fork were fused to make one wider prong that acted as a cutting edge. Like tea knives and silver teaspoons, the forks usually came in little boxes of six.

For the cake
2 eggs
⅔ cup light soft brown sugar
5 tbsp oil (sunflower, vegetable or corn)
Generous ¾ cup self-rising flour, sifted
1½ cups grated carrot
1 tsp ground cinnamon
Scant ½ cup shredded coconut

For the topping
⅓ cup cream cheese
¾ stick butter
½ cup confectioners' sugar
Grated rind of 1 lime
Toasted coconut and grated lime, to decorate (optional)

1 Preheat the oven to 375°F. Grease and line a 2 lb loaf pan or a 7 in round cake pan.

2 Beat together the eggs and sugar until very creamy. Add the oil and beat hard. Fold in the remaining ingredients and turn into the prepared pan. Smooth the top, then slightly hollow out the middle to avoid a very domed top on the finished cake. Bake for 35–40 minutes until golden and well risen and a skewer comes out clean.

3 Remove the cake from the oven and turn out onto a wire rack to cool. To make the topping, beat the ingredients together until light and creamy and spread over the top of the cake. Make a pattern with the prongs of a fork.

For a more traditional carrot cake simply leave the lime and coconut out of the topping.

Sticky Lemon Cake

Makes 1 2 lb loaf or 7 in round cake

This wonderfully tangy cake is a recipe from Castle Drogo in Devon which was built by Julius Drewe in 1900 to Sir Edwin Lutyens' design. Mr Drewe opened his own tea store (The Willow Pattern Tea Store) in 1878, then set up the Home and Colonial Stores in 1883 and sold so much tea that he became a millionaire. While he lived at Castle Drogo, tea was served each day in the library and was "a wonderful meal with wafer-thin bread and butter, scones and jam and Devonshire cream—and cakes in great variety, followed by whatever fruit was in season".

For the cake
1 stick butter, softened
½ cup superfine sugar
2 eggs
Generous ¾ cup self-rising flour, sifted
Grated rind and juice of ½ lemon
1½ tbsp confectioners' sugar, sifted

For the frosting
½–¾ cup confectioners' sugar, sifted
Juice and finely grated rind of ½ lemon

1   Preheat the oven to 325°F. Grease and line a 2 lb loaf pan or a 7 in round pan. Beat together the butter and sugar until light and fluffy. Beat in the eggs, one at a time, whisking hard after the addition of each one.

2   Fold in the flour and rind, mix well and turn into the prepared pan. Bake for around 45 minutes or until a skewer comes out clean.

3   Remove from the oven and make several holes in the top of the cake with a skewer. Mix together the confectioners' sugar and lemon juice and pour gently over the cake. Leave in the pan until absolutely cold.

4   Meanwhile, make the frosting. Mix together the confectioners' sugar, lemon rind and juice. When the cake is cold, turn out and frost with the prepared mixture.

Chocolate Orange Drizzle Cake

Makes 1 2 lb loaf or 7 in round cake

Chocolate cakes are wonderful accompanied by a strong, black tea such as Kenya or a strong Ceylon or Assam. Brew the tea for 4–5 minutes to make sure that all the flavor and goodness are drawn out into the boiling water. Stronger teas often drink well with a little milk so try adding a small quantity of two percent/semi-skimmed, which works best in tea.

For the cake
1½ sticks butter, softened
¾ cup superfine sugar
3 large eggs
Grated rind of 2 oranges
1¼ cups self-rising flour, sifted
2 tbsp milk

For the topping
Juice of 2 oranges
½ cup granulated sugar
2 oz semisweet chocolate

1   Preheat the oven to 350°F. Grease and line a 2 lb loaf pan or a 7 in round pan. Cream together the butter and sugar until light and fluffy. Add the eggs, one at a time, and beat well.

2   Add the grated orange rind, flour and milk and fold in with a metal spoon. Turn into the prepared pan, smooth the top and bake for 30–40 minutes until a skewer comes out clean.

3   Remove the cake from the oven and leave to cool in the pan. When cool, score the top of the cake lightly with a sharp knife.

4   Put the orange juice and granulated sugar into a pan and heat gently until the sugar has dissolved. Bring to a boil and boil for 1–2 minutes. Pour over the cake.

5   When all the juice has soaked in, carefully remove the cake from the pan. Melt the chocolate and drizzle over the top in criss-cross lines, or in any pattern of your choice.

Regional
Cakes

Suffolk Fourses

During the harvest each year in England's eastern counties, the farmers' wives worked hard to produce four or five meals a day to feed the hungry local and itinerant workers. Flasks of tea and bottles of cold homemade lemonade were carried out in bags and baskets by the women and children for the midday and mid-afternoon meals. Everyone stopped work, found somewhere to rest in the shade of a nearby haystack and devoured the freshly baked breads, rolls and cakes.

1 oz fresh yeast (to substitute dried yeast, see page 36)
1 tsp superfine sugar
1¼ cups milk
6½ cups all-purpose flour, sifted
½ tsp salt
¼ cup shortening, e.g. Crisco, softened
½ cup superfine , granulated or demerara sugar
½ cup currants or raisins
A pinch of mixed spice
1½ sticks butter
3 eggs, well beaten
Superfine or demerara sugar for dredging

1   Cream the yeast with 1 tsp of superfine sugar. Warm the milk and add to the yeast. Mix together the flour and salt and rub in the fat. Add the sugar, currants or raisins and spice and mix well.

2   Melt the butter and stir into the beaten eggs. Add to the milk and yeast mixture and pour into the flour. Mix with a round-bladed knife to a light dough. Cover the bowl with a clean damp cloth and leave in a warm place for about 2 hours until the dough has doubled in size.

3   Meanwhile, grease two baking sheets. When the dough has risen knead on a lightly floured board, then roll out to a thickness of ¾ in and cut into circles 4 in in diameter. Place on the prepared sheets and leave to rise in a warm place for 30 minutes.

4   Preheat the oven to 400°F. When the fourses have risen, mark the tops into four sections and dredge with superfine or demerara sugar. Bake for 15–20 minutes until firm and golden. Remove from the oven and eat either warm or cold, split and buttered.

Bath Buns

In the 18th century, these local treats were flavored with sherry, rose water and caraway seeds. The more modern version uses candied citrus peel and currants and is topped with the characteristic crushed lump sugar which gives the buns their distinctive crunchy quality.

1 oz fresh yeast (to substitute dried yeast, see page 36)
½ cup superfine sugar
4 cups white bread flour, sifted
⅔ cup milk, warmed
A pinch of salt
Scant 1 cup currants and golden raisins, mixed
Scant ½ cup mixed candied peel
¼ cup butter, melted
2 eggs, beaten
Crushed sugar lump for sprinkling

1 In a medium-sized bowl, cream the yeast with 1 tsp of the sugar. Add ⅔ cup of the flour and the warmed milk and mix to a thick batter. Leave in a warm place for 15–20 minutes until frothy.

2 Mix together the remaining flour and the salt. Add the remaining superfine sugar, currants, golden raisins and peel. Add to the yeast mixture with the melted butter and most of the beaten eggs (reserving a little for glazing) and mix to a soft dough. Knead on a floured board for 2–3 minutes until smooth.

3 Place the dough in a lightly floured bowl, cover with a damp cloth and leave in a warm place to rise for 1½–1¾ hours until doubled in size.

4 Grease two baking sheets. Knock back the dough and form into bun shapes, each weighing about 2½ oz. Place well apart on the prepared sheets, cover with oiled plastic wrap and leave to rise for about 30 minutes until doubled in size.

5 Preheat the oven to 375°F. Glaze the buns with the remaining beaten egg and sprinkle with the crushed sugar. Bake for 15 minutes until well risen and golden. Remove from the oven and lift onto a wire rack to cool.

Cornish Splits

Eaten as an alternative to scones, the recipe for these splits comes from Lanhydrock, originally built in the 17th century but partly destroyed by fire and rebuilt in the 19th century. Cooks and maids in its vast kitchens would have busied themselves regularly making bread, splits, cakes and cookies to satisfy the family's teatime requirements. In the morning room each day, a table is covered with a lace cloth and set ready for tea with French china teacups and saucers, silver tea knives and teaspoons, small linen napkins, a beehive honey pot, a silver jam pot and a silver butter dish.

2 oz fresh yeast (to substitute dried yeast, see page 36)
Scant ¼ cup superfine sugar
Just under 1⅓ cups warm milk and water, mixed
6½ cups white bread flour, sifted
1 egg, beaten

1 Grease two baking sheets. Mix together the yeast, sugar and warm milk and water. Leave in a warm place for about 20–30 minutes until frothy.

2 Add the liquid to the flour with the beaten egg and mix to a soft dough. Knead until smooth and elastic. Leave in a warm place for about an hour until doubled in size.

3 Knock back the dough, knead again and divide into 3 oz pieces. Mold with your hands into neat bun shapes, place on the prepared sheets and leave in a warm place for about 20 minutes until well risen.

4 Preheat the oven to 325°F. When the splits are well risen, bake for 20–25 minutes until they just start to turn brown. Remove from the oven and cool on a wire rack. To serve, split and fill with jam and clotted cream and dust the tops with confectioners' sugar.

Cherry Bakewells

Bakewell tarts descend from what were originally called Bakewell puddings, said to date back to the 16th century and to have been invented by accident when a cook at a local inn misunderstood her employer's instructions to make a strawberry tart. Apparently, instead of adding eggs and sugar to the pastry, she beat them up with a secret ingredient and spread the mixture over the strawberries. Today, the recipe calls for strawberry jam instead of fresh fruit and sometimes decorates the top with a little frosting and a cherry.

8 oz shortcrust pastry (see page 59)
Scant ¼ cup strawberry jam
1 stick butter, softened
½ cup superfine sugar
2 eggs
½ cup ground almonds
⅓ cup self-rising flour, sifted
1 tsp almond essence
1½ cups confectioners' sugar, sifted
1–2 tbsp water
20 cherries (fresh, stoned or candied)

1 Make the pastry according to the instructions on page 59 and chill for at least 15 minutes.

2 Preheat the oven to 400°F. Grease 20 patty pans. On a lightly floured board, roll out the pastry and cut twenty circles using a 3 in/7.5 cm cutter. Use to line the prepared pans and spread a little jam in the base of each.

3 Beat together the butter and superfine sugar, then beat in the eggs, one at a time, adding half the ground almonds after each one. Add the flour and almond essence and stir well.

4 Spoon the batter into the pastry cases and bake for 20 minutes until well risen, firm and golden. Remove from the oven and leave to cool in the pans.

5 Mix together the confectioners' sugar and water and, when the tarts are cold, spoon the frosting on the top. Decorate each with a cherry.

18th-Century Pepper Cake

Although generally used in savory dishes, black pepper is sometimes added to cakes with ginger and other spices. Some recipes for this traditional Westmorland fruit cake also add dates and walnuts but this one from Wordsworth House in the Lake District uses cloves, currants, raisins and peel.

Scant 3¼ cups all-purpose flour, sifted
1 tsp baking powder
1 stick butter, softened
1 cup superfine sugar
Generous ¾ cup currants
²/₃ cup raisins
Scant ¼ cup mixed candied peel
½ tsp ground cloves
½ tsp ground ginger
½ tsp ground black pepper
²/₃ cup molasses
4 eggs, beaten

1 Preheat the oven to 300°F. Grease and line a 9 in round, deep cake pan. Mix together the flour and baking powder and rub in the butter until the mixture resembles fine breadcrumbs. Add all the other ingredients and mix to a thick batter.

2 Turn the batter into the prepared pan and bake for 2 hours until a skewer comes out clean. Remove from the oven and leave to cool in the pan for 15 minutes before turning out onto a wire rack to cool completely. When cool, wrap in foil or plastic wrap and store for a few days before eating.

Welsh Cakes

The most famous of traditional cakes from Wales, these little flat spicy griddle cakes were offered to visitors calling at the house. Welsh cakes were traditionally cooked on a bakestone that sat on the open kitchen fire. Their name in Welsh is pice ary maen which literally means "cakes on the stone". Two variations are cooked today—Llech Cymreig is made with all-purpose flour to give a flatter, crisper cake, and Jam Split is made by cutting the Welsh cake across the middle and filling it with jam.

1²/₃ cups self-rising flour, sifted
A pinch of salt
2 oz shortening, e.g. Crisco, softened
½ stick butter, softened
Generous ⅓ cup granulated sugar
Scant ¼ cup currants
½ egg, beaten
1½ tbsp milk
Superfine sugar for sprinkling

1 Preheat a griddle or a heavy frying pan to a moderate, even temperature. Mix together the flour and salt and rub in the fat. Add the sugar and currants and mix with the egg and milk to a soft dough.

2 On a floured board, roll out to a thickness of ¼–½ in and cut out circles using a 3 in cutter. Place on the griddle and cook both sides until light golden. Lift onto a wire rack to cool and sprinkle with superfine sugar before serving.

Welsh Cakes are quick to make and taste wonderful served warm from the griddle with a steaming cup of tea.

Banbury Cakes

Banbury cakes date back to pagan days and are thought to have been eaten at May Day celebrations. Recipes have changed greatly over the centuries, varying from a type of fruited bread flavored with caraway seeds, to pastry cases filled with fruit, saffron and sherry. Today's cakes are a fruit-filled pastry with a flaky outer case and plump dried fruit inside.

12 oz puff pastry
(see page 58)
½ stick butter
Generous ¾ cup currants
Generous ⅓ cup mixed candied peel
¼ tsp ground cinnamon
½ tsp allspice or grated nutmeg
2½ tbsp light or dark soft brown
sugar
1 tbsp dark rum
A little milk or water
1 egg white, lightly beaten
Superfine sugar to dredge

1 Make the pastry according to the instructions on page 58 and chill for at least 30 minutes.

2 Melt the butter in a small pan and add the dried fruit, spices, brown sugar and rum. Stir and leave to cool.

3 Preheat the oven to 450°F. Grease two baking sheets. On a lightly floured board, roll out the pastry to a thickness of ¼ in and cut into circles about 4 in in diameter.

4 Place a spoonful of the fruit mixture on each circle, dampen the edges of the pastry with a little milk or water and gather the edges together. Seal well, turn each cake over and roll gently to a neat oval shape. Cut three slashes in the top and place on the prepared baking sheets.

5 Brush the tops with the beaten egg white and dredge with superfine sugar. Bake for 10–15 minutes until golden. Remove from the oven and lift onto a wire rack to cool slightly before serving.

Kedleston Marmalade Cake

Marmalades started life as a sort of quince (marmelo) jam but, in the 17th century, were made in England with oranges instead. The bittersweet flavor adds an interesting bite to this cake which goes very well with Ceylon or Assam tea.

1½ sticks butter, softened
⅓ cup light or dark soft brown sugar
4 tbsp corn syrup
2 eggs
Scant ½ cup orange marmalade
1⅔ cups self-rising whole-wheat flour, sifted
2 tsp baking powder
½ tsp ground ginger
3–4 tbsp orange juice

1 Preheat the oven to 350°F. Grease and line an 8 in round pan. Beat together the butter and sugar until light and fluffy. Add the syrup and beat again.

2 Whisk together the eggs and marmalade and add to the mixture with the flour, baking powder and ginger. Stir in the orange juice to give a soft, dropping consistency.

3 Turn the batter into the prepared pan and bake for about 1 hour until a skewer comes out clean. Remove from the oven and leave to cool in the pan for 15 minutes before turning out onto a wire rack to cool completely.

If you want to dress this cake up try making an orange glacé frosting to drizzle over the top.

Ultimate Tarts

The tart is another British teatime staple, and every region has its own take on a pastry case filled with something sweet and delicious.

Treacle tart
Serves 12

Beningbrough Hall near York serves this sticky, indulgent tart in its tearoom. The house, built in 1716, has a closet on the ground floor as part of a grand suite of rooms used by honored guests. Always richly decorated, the closet was often used to entertain visitors to tea and all the essential porcelain teapots, bowls and dishes required to brew and serve tea were displayed on shelves and stepped ledges over the fireplace. The tea was too expensive to leave in charge of the servants so it was also kept here in little porcelain jars imported from China. The jars gradually changed shape and became squat, hinge-lidded tea caddies.

For the pastry
¼ cup shortening, e.g. Crisco, softened
½ stick butter, softened
1⅔ cups all-purpose flour, sifted
2 tbsp superfine sugar
A little cold water

For the filling
1 lb corn syrup
2–3 cups fresh white breadcrumbs
Juice of ½ lemon

1 Make the pastry by rubbing the fats into the flour. Add the sugar and enough water to mix to a soft but pliable dough. Knead lightly, wrap in plastic wrap and chill for at least 15 minutes.

2 Preheat the oven to 350°F. Grease a 10 in round flan dish. On a floured board, roll out the pastry to fit the prepared dish and use to line the base and sides.

3 Place the syrup in a pan and warm gently. Remove from the heat, add the breadcrumbs and lemon juice and leave until the bread is well soaked. If the mixture is dry, add a little more syrup. Turn the mixture into the pastry case and spread evenly. Bake for 25–30 minutes until the pastry is golden and the filling nicely browned. Remove from the oven and serve warm or cold.

Yorkshire curd tart
Makes 1 x 8 in round tart

Open curd cheese tarts and cheesecakes have been favorite puddings in Yorkshire for centuries and were often served as Easter specialties to use up some of the plentiful eggs and curd cheese available after the Lenten fast.

6 oz shortcrust pastry
(see page 59)
½ stick butter, softened
¼ cup superfine sugar
1 egg, beaten
Scant ½ cup currants
½ cup curd cheese
1 cup sponge or cookie crumbs
Grated rind and juice of 1 lemon
½ tsp grated nutmeg

1 Make the pastry according to the instructions on page 59 and chill for at least 15 minutes. Preheat the oven to 375°F. Grease an 8 in round flan dish or pan. On a floured board, roll out the pastry to fit the dish and use to line the base and sides.

2 Beat together the butter and sugar until light and fluffy. Add the beaten egg and beat hard. Add the currants, cheese, sponge or cookie crumbs, lemon rind and juice and the nutmeg and beat again. Turn into the pastry case, smooth and bake for 20–25 minutes until golden. Serve warm or cold with cream.

Longshaw tart
Serves 20

Named after the estate near Sheffield where this recipe comes from, the tart is a version of Bakewell tart, another local specialty. This may well have featured on the "high tea" table when the family arrived home hungry at the end of the working day. Whereas "afternoon tea" was also called "low tea" (because one sat in low armchairs and chaises longues) or "handed tea" (because the cups of tea were handed around by the hostess), "high tea" was called "meat tea" and "great tea".

12 oz shortcrust pastry
(see page 59)
6–7 tbsp jam (raspberry, strawberry or apricot)
2¼ sticks butter, softened
Generous 1 cup granulated sugar
Generous 1 cup peanuts, finely chopped
2¼ cups fresh breadcrumbs (white or whole-wheat)
3 eggs, beaten
1½ tsp almond essence

1 Make the pastry according to the instructions on page 59 and chill for at least 15 minutes. Preheat the oven to 375°F. Grease a 10 x 12 x 1½in pan. On a floured board, roll out the pastry to make a rectangle to fit the pan and use to line the base.

2 Spread the jam over the pastry. Beat together the butter and sugar until light and fluffy. Add the rest of the ingredients and mix well. Turn into the pastry case and bake for 25–30 minutes until firm and golden. Remove from the oven and leave to cool in the pan. When cold, cut into slices and lift carefully out of the pan.

Secretary tarts
Makes 24 individual tarts

These oddly named tartlets are served in the tearoom at Polesden Lacey in Surrey—a Regency house with strong links to afternoon tea rituals. Hosted by Mrs Ronnie Greville, the elegant but renowned society hostess, tea was an important part of the famous parties held from 1906 until the outbreak of World War II. Guests included Indian maharajahs, literary figures such as Beverley Nichols and Harold Nicolson, prominent politicians and royalty, including Edward VII and the honeymooning future George VI and Queen Elizabeth.

1 lb rich shortcrust or shortcrust pastry (see page 59)
1½ sticks butter
Generous ¾ cup light soft brown sugar
1 x 14 oz can condensed milk
½ cup walnuts, roughly chopped
⅓ cup raisins

1 Make the pastry according to the instructions on page 59 and chill for at least 15 minutes. Preheat the oven to 450°F. Grease 24 patty pans.

2 On a floured board, roll out the pastry to a thickness of ¼ in and cut 24 circles using a 3 in fluted cutter. Use to line the prepared patty pans. Place little squares of greaseproof paper in each tart and fill with baking beans. Bake blind for 10 minutes.

3 Remove the pastry cases from the oven, lift the baking beans and paper out of the cases and return to the oven for a further 5 minutes. Remove and turn off the oven.

4 Put the butter, sugar and milk into a medium-sized pan and bring to a boil. Boil hard for 7 minutes, stirring all the time, until the mixture becomes a caramel color. Remove from the heat and allow to cool for 5 minutes. Stir in the walnuts and raisins and spoon into the pastry cases. Put into the refrigerator to set. Serve cold.

Most tart recipes can be adapted to make dainty little individual tarts rather than large tarts that need to be cut into wedges. Just watch the baking time and oven temperature—you may need to reduce both slightly in order to cook the tartlets properly.

Lancaster lemon tart
Makes 1 x 8 in round tart

Today we take afternoon tea at 4 or 5 o'clock but in the early days of tea drinking in England, tea was served as an after-dinner "digestif". When the last morsels of food had been consumed, the company would retire to a drawing room where the tea table had been prepared by the servants.

6 oz shortcrust pastry
(see page 59)
½ cup lemon curd
1 stick butter, softened
½ cup superfine sugar
2 eggs, beaten
3 tsp lemon juice
Generous ½ cup self-rising flour, sifted
Scant ¼ cup ground almonds

1 Make the pastry according to the instructions on page 59 and chill for at least 15 minutes. Preheat the oven to 350°F. Grease an 8 in loose-bottomed round flan dish.

2 On a floured board, roll out the pastry and use to line the dish. Spread the lemon curd over the base. Beat together the butter and sugar until pale and fluffy. Gradually add the beaten eggs and the lemon juice and beat well. Add the flour and ground almonds and fold in with a metal spoon.

3 Spread the batter over the lemon curd and smooth out. Bake for 35 minutes, then reduce the oven temperature to 300°F and bake for 10–15 minutes more until the sponge springs back when lightly pressed. Remove from the oven and leave to cool in the dish. When cold, cut into pieces and serve.

Norfolk tart
Makes 1 x 7 in round tart

Norfolk is more famous for its use of honey in desserts and cakes than for syrup, but this syrup and cream-based recipe makes a delicious teatime treat.

6 oz rich shortcrust pastry
(see page 59)
⅓ cup corn syrup
1 tbsp butter
Grated rind of ½ lemon
2 tbsp heavy cream
1 egg

1 Make the pastry according to the instructions on page 59 and chill for at least 15 minutes. Preheat the oven to 400°F. Grease a 7in round flan dish.

2 On a floured board, roll out the pastry to make a circle and use to line the prepared pan or dish. Bake blind for 15–20 minutes. Remove from the oven and lift out the baking beans and paper. Reduce the oven temperature to 350°F.

3 Warm the syrup in a pan with the butter and lemon rind until the butter has dissolved. Beat the cream and egg together and add to the mixture. Pour into the pastry case and bake for 20 minutes until golden and firm. Remove from the oven and serve warm or cold.

Lakeland coconut tart
Makes 1 x 8 in round tart

This recipe comes from Quarry Bank Mill in Cheshire which thrived as a result of the burgeoning cotton industry of the 18th century. The staple diet of an average worker was potatoes and wheaten bread, washed down with tea or coffee. The Comte de la Rochefoucauld, while touring in England in 1784, wrote, "Throughout the whole of England the drinking of tea is general. You have it twice a day and though the expense is considerable, the humblest peasant has his tea twice a day just like the rich man".

6 oz shortcrust pastry
(see page 59)
3–4 tbsp strawberry or raspberry jam
1 stick butter
¼ cup superfine sugar
2 level tbsp corn syrup
2¼ cups shredded coconut
2 eggs, beaten

1 Make the pastry according to the instructions on page 59 and chill for at least 15 minutes. Preheat the oven to 375°F. Grease an 8 in round flan dish or a deep pie plate.

2 On a floured board, roll out the pastry and use to line the prepared dish. Spread the jam over the pastry base.

3 Melt together the butter, sugar and syrup and stir in the coconut and beaten eggs. Turn into the pastry case and bake in the middle of the oven for 30 minutes until golden, covering with foil after the first 10 minutes of baking time. Remove from the oven and leave to cool in the dish.

Manchester tart
Makes 1 x 8 in round tart

This meringue-topped tart is a little like a Queen of Puddings in a pastry shell. The recipe comes from Dunham Massey in Cheshire where the "tearoom" in the house holds rare tea and coffee tables, the family silver teawares and two tall tea caddies of japanned metal inlaid with mother of pearl. These large tins would have held the main supply of loose-leaf tea and smaller caddies, now on show on side tables and mantel shelves in the drawing and dining rooms, would have been regularly replenished.

6 oz flaky pastry (see page 58)
3–4 tbsp raspberry or strawberry jam
Rind of 1 lemon, cut into strips
1¼ cups milk
1 cup fresh breadcrumbs
½ stick butter, softened
2 eggs, separated
Generous ⅓ cup superfine sugar
1 tbsp brandy
Superfine sugar for dredging

1 Make the pastry according to the instructions on page 58 and chill for at least 45 minutes. Preheat the oven to 375°F. Grease and line an 8 in round pie dish or loose-bottomed round pan.

2 On a floured board, roll out the pastry and use to line the dish. Spread the jam over the base.

3 Put the lemon rind and milk into a pan and bring to a boil. Strain onto the breadcrumbs and leave for 5 minutes. Add the butter, egg yolks, 2 tbsp of the sugar and the brandy and beat well. Pour into the pastry case and bake for 45 minutes.

4 Whisk the egg whites until stiff and fold in the remaining ⅓ cup of the sugar. Remove the tart from the oven and spread the meringue over the filling. Dredge with superfine sugar and bake for 15 minutes until the meringue is brown. Remove from the oven and cool. Serve with cream.

Scones
&
Slices

Florentine Slice

This rich, chocolate slice is made to a recipe from Kingston Lacy in Dorset, once the home of the Bankes family. Margaret Bankes, who lived there in the 17th and 18th century, began buying teaware for the house and between 1701 and 1710, she acquired various "setts of tea dishes and saucers", "a kenester", "a china sugar dish", a pair of tea tongs and 10 teapots. She also purchased "a black Japan table for my closet" (where she took tea) and four more tea tables.

12 oz good quality semisweet chocolate
2 cups mixed dried fruit (raisins, golden raisins, currants, peel)
⅔ cup candied cherries
Generous 1 cup shredded coconut
½ cup superfine sugar
½ cup butter, melted
2 eggs, beaten

1 Line an 8 x 11 in pan with foil. Melt the chocolate and spread evenly in the base of the pan. Leave to cool in the refrigerator until set.

2 Preheat the oven to 350°F. Mix together the dried fruit, candied cherries, coconut, sugar, butter and beaten eggs and spread evenly over the chocolate. Bake for 25 minutes until golden brown. Remove from the oven and leave to cool in the pan.

3 When cool, place the pan in the refrigerator until really cold. Cut into oblong slices and turn out of the pan.

This rich, gooey slice contains no flour, so is ideal for people who cannot eat wheat.

Apricot Sesame Slice

As well as adding their distinctive flavor and aroma to foods, sesame seeds are rich in minerals and vitamins and also have antioxidant properties. They marry very well with the apricots in this recipe.

For the base
1 stick butter
⅓ cup corn syrup
⅔ cup demerara sugar
2⅔ cup porridge oats
Generous 1 cup shredded coconut
½ cup sesame seeds, untoasted
3 tsp ground cinnamon
A pinch of salt
⅔ cup dried apricots, roughly chopped
4 oz chocolate chips (semisweet)

For the topping
¼ cup sesame seeds, untoasted

1 Preheat the oven to 150°C, 300°F, gas mark 2. Grease an 8 x 11 in pan.

2 Melt the butter and syrup together in a large pan. Add the sugar, oats, coconut, sesame seeds, cinnamon, salt and apricots and stir well, making sure that all the ingredients are evenly distributed. Stir in the chocolate chips and mix thoroughly.

3 Turn the mixture into the prepared pan and press down firmly. Smooth the top and sprinkle with the ¼ cup sesame seeds. Press well into the mixture and bake for 30–35 minutes until golden and firm. Remove from the oven and leave to cool in the pan. When cold, cut into slices or squares.

Sweetmince Squares

Filled with a sort of mincemeat mixture, this Irish recipe includes cinnamon and ginger. Under the rule of the Portuguese and then the Dutch, the island of Sri Lanka was once the world's main producer of cinnamon. Ginger has all sorts of health benefits. It can help ease nausea, reduce inflammation, settle the digestion, and minimize pain from arthritis. Both spices are also commonly used as additional flavorings for tea, added to the tea after it has been manufactured.

1½ lb rich shortcrust pastry (see page 59)
1½ tsp cornstarch
½ tsp custard powder
¾ cup water
1 cup currants and raisins
Scant ½ cup mixed candied peel
Scant ½ cup granulated sugar
1 tsp ground cinnamon
1 tsp mixed spice
½ tsp ground ginger
A little water or milk
Superfine sugar for dredging

1 Make the pastry according to the instructions on page 59 and chill for at least 15 minutes. Preheat the oven to 350°F. Grease a 7 x 11 in jellyroll pan.

2 On a floured board, roll out half the pastry and use it to line the prepared pan.

3 Mix together the cornstarch and custard powder with the water and put in a pan with the water, currants and raisins, candied peel, granulated sugar, cinnamon, mixed spice and ginger. Bring to a boil and simmer until thick.

4 Gently tip the sweetmince mixture into the pastry case and spread evenly with the back of a spoon.

5 Roll out the remaining pastry and lay on top. Wet the edges of the pastry with a little water or milk and press together well. Bake for 45–50 minutes until golden. Remove from the oven and dredge with superfine sugar. Allow to cool in the tin. When cold, cut into squares and serve.

Ginger & Treacle Scones

From Wimpole Hall in Cambridgeshire comes this spicy, richly dark scone recipe. To ensure a regular supply of quality loose leaf tea during the years of rationing that followed World War II, the Bambridge family who lived at Wimpole Hall entrusted its entire stock of tea coupons to Twinings tea company. From 1950 to 1953 further orders for Indian tea were placed with Twinings and the tea usually arrived in 14-lb cases or sometimes in 5-lb packets. The various tea caddies displayed around the house would once have been regularly filled from a large lockable storage bin kept in the housekeeper's dry store in the basement.

1²/₃ cups self-rising flour, sifted
1½ tsp baking powder
2 tsp ground ginger
½ stick butter, softened and cut into small pieces
6 tbsp milk
1 rounded tbsp molasses
A little milk for glazing

1 Preheat the oven to 425°F. Grease a baking sheet. Mix together the flour, baking powder and ginger and rub in the fat until the mixture resembles breadcrumbs.

2 Warm the milk and molasses together in a small pan until lukewarm. Add to the mixture and mix with a round-bladed knife to a soft dough.

3 On a lightly floured board, knead the dough until smooth, then roll out to a thickness of ¾ in. Cut into circles using a 2 in cutter and place on the prepared sheet.

4 Brush the tops with a little milk. Bake just above the center of the oven for 10–15 minutes until well risen and golden brown. Remove from the oven and lift onto a wire rack to cool. Serve warm or cold with butter.

Cherry & Almond Scones

Makes
20

From Rufford Old Hall in Lancashire comes the recipe for scones subtly flavored with a hint of almonds. Although it was built in the early 15th century, long before the English learnt about tea, the house has many interesting tea-related items including various unusual teapots and a large ornate "teapoy". Intended to double as a small tea table and as a box that contained the tea, its name does not derive from "tea" but from Hindi tipai meaning three-footed, since its sturdy leg usually ended in three carved feet.

3¼ cups self-rising flour, sifted
½ tsp baking powder
1 stick butter, softened
Generous ⅓ cup superfine sugar
Scant 1 cup candied cherries, roughly chopped
1 egg, beaten
A few drops of almond essence
About ¾ cup milk

1   Preheat the oven to 350°F. Grease two baking sheets. Mix together the flour and baking powder and rub in the butter. Add the sugar, cherries, beaten egg, almond essence and enough milk to give a soft but not sticky dough. Knead lightly until smooth.

2   On a floured board, roll out to a thickness of ½ in and cut out circles using a 2 in cutter. Place on the prepared sheets and bake for 20–25 minutes until well risen, firm and golden. Remove from the oven and lift onto a wire rack to cool. Serve with butter or clotted cream and jam.

A delicious variation on the classic scone recipe, candied cherries and almond essence are a match made in heaven.

Ultimate Scones!

Delicious served with a large dollop of clotted cream and tangy strawberry jam, these scone recipes are guaranteed to get your mouth watering and your tastebuds tingling!

Eggless scones
Makes 12

The name for scones seems to descend from Dutch schoonbrot or German sconbrot meaning fine bread, and they seem to have become part of afternoon tea menus in the latter half of the 19th century.

½ stick butter, softened
¼ cup shortening, e.g. Crisco, softened
2½ cups self-rising flour, sifted
½–⅔ cup milk

1 Preheat the oven to 375°F. Grease two baking sheets. Rub the butter and shortening into the flour, working as quickly and lightly as possible with cold hands. Add enough milk to give a soft, bread-like dough.

2 On a floured board, roll out to a thickness of ¾ in and cut into circles with a 2½ in cutter. Place on the prepared sheets and bake for 15–20 minutes until lightly golden and well risen. Remove from the oven and lift onto a wire rack to cool. These plain, light, well-risen scones are perfect served warm with jam and Cornish clotted cream.

Welsh cheese & herb scones
Makes 12

Obviously not intended to be eaten with clotted cream, savory scones make a satisfying part of high tea. This recipe comes from Penrhyn Castle in Wales which inexplicably has a Russian samovar on display.

3¼ cups self-rising flour, sifted
1 tsp salt
1 stick butter, softened
1 tsp mixed dried herbs
2 cups grated Cheddar or other strong cheese
8 tbsp milk
8 tbsp water

1 Preheat the oven to 425°F. Grease a baking sheet. Mix together the flour and salt and rub in the butter. Add the herbs and 1¼ cups of the cheese. Add the milk and water and mix to a soft dough.

2 On a floured board, roll out to a thickness of 1 in and cut into circles using a 2½ in cutter. Place on the prepared sheet, top each scone with a little of the remaining grated cheese and bake for 10–15 minutes until golden. Remove from the oven and lift onto a wire rack to cool slightly. Serve warm or cold with butter.

Clotted cream is a thick cream made by heating full-fat cow's milk indirectly, using a water bath or steam, and then leaving it in shallow pans to cool slowly. As it cools, the cream forms "clots". The cream is usually assocoated with the south-west of England, in particular the counties of Cornwall and Devon.

Fruit scones
Makes 14–16 scones

The recipe for these delicious scones comes from Little Moreton Hall in Cheshire which was built in the late 16th century, about 100 years before the first tea arrived in England. They are the ultimate English treat.

3¼ cups self-rising flour, sifted
A pinch of salt
½ tsp baking powder
1 stick butter, softened
1½ tbsp superfine sugar
1½ tbsp raisins or golden raisins
Scant 1¼ cups milk

1 Preheat the oven to 425°F. Grease two baking sheets.

2 Mix together the flour, salt and baking powder and rub in the butter. Add the sugar and raisins and mix with enough milk to give a soft dough.

3 On a floured board, roll out to a thickness of ¾ in and cut into circles using a 2½ in cutter. Place on the prepared sheets and bake for 13–15 minutes until golden and firm. Remove from the oven and lift onto a wire rack to cool. Serve warm or cold with butter.

All kinds of dried fruit may be incorporated successfully into scones. Try cranberries with a little grated orange or lime zest, or you could go for a tropical feel with mango, papaya and pineapple, adding in some spice such as ginger if you like.

Irish honey scones
Makes 1 x 7 in round

Should clotted cream go on the scone before or after the jelly? It depends on where the scone is being eaten. In Devon cream goes first because it is possible to get more cream to stay on the scone! In Cornwall, jam goes first. Which way is "correct" is a debate that has been raging for centuries between the two counties.

⅔ cup all-purpose whole-wheat flour
Generous ¾ cup all-purpose white flour, sifted
2 tsp baking powder
A pinch of salt
¾ stick butter, softened
1 tbsp light soft brown sugar
2 tbsp clear honey
¼–⅓ cup milk

1 Preheat the oven to 400°F. Grease a baking sheet.

2 Mix together the flours, baking powder and salt and rub in the butter. Add the sugar and mix. Mix the honey with the milk and stir until the honey has dissolved. Reserve a little for glazing and add the rest to the flour. Mix to a soft dough.

3 Place the dough on the prepared sheet and shape with the hands into a flat circle approximately 7 in in diameter. Divide the top into eight wedges.

4 Bake for 15–20 minutes. Remove from the oven, glaze the top with the honey and milk mixture and return to the oven for a further 5–10 minutes until golden. Remove from the oven and serve warm with jam and cream or butter.

Making one large scone disc instead of small individual ones is possible with all types of scone dough, as long as you make the dough an even thickness.

Teabreads & Loaves

Herb Bread

This herby, cheesy bread packs a real punch of flavor. You can vary the herbs according to what's growing in your garden, what you're serving the bread with or what kind of cheese you're going to use. Equally, you can alter the type of cheese to suit your taste—as long as it's got plenty of flavor it's sure to be delicious.

1²/₃ cups self-rising flour (white or a mixture of half white and half whole-wheat), sifted
1 tsp dry English mustard powder
2 tbsp fresh chopped herbs (chives, thyme, basil, sage, parsley)
1 cup mature Cheddar cheese, grated
¼ stick butter
1 egg, beaten
²/₃ cup water

1 Preheat the oven to 375°F. Grease a 1 lb loaf pan.

2 Mix together the flour, mustard, herbs and cheese. Melt the butter, add to the mixture with the egg and water and mix to a soft, wet, cake-like dough.

3 Turn into the prepared pan and bake for 45 minutes until well risen and golden brown. Remove from the oven and cool on a wire rack. Serve warm or cold with butter.

Serve it as the savory element to afternoon tea in thin slices spread with butter, or pack it as part of a delicious summer picnic.

Date & Walnut Loaf

Makes 1 2 lb loaf

This Cornish recipe from Cotehele in Cornwall is typical in its use of spices, brown sugar and exotic fruit. From the 17th century, ships from the Orient imported such luxuries through the Cornish ports and many cake recipes from the region include ginger, cinnamon, nutmeg, dried dates and raisins. Cotehele would certainly have known about such ingredients, sitting as it does close to the River Tamar which for centuries was the only effective route to the outside world. The immense oven in the north wall of the kitchen almost certainly baked a number of these loaves over the centuries.

1²/₃ cups self-rising flour, sifted
½ cup walnut halves
1 tsp mixed spice
¾ stick butter
²/₃ cup light or dark soft brown sugar
8 oz whole dates
²/₃ cup water
2 eggs, beaten
2 tbsp sesame seeds

1 Preheat the oven to 350°F. Grease and line a 2 lb loaf pan. Mix together the flour, walnuts and mixed spice.

2 Place the butter, sugar, dates and water in a pan and bring gently to the boil. Remove from the heat and cool for a few minutes. Add to the flour, spice and nuts with the beaten eggs and beat well.

3 Turn into the prepared pan, hollow the middle a little and sprinkle the top with the sesame seeds. Bake for 1–1¼ hours until a skewer comes out clean. Remove from the oven and turn out onto a wire rack to cool. Serve sliced with butter.

Blackberry Teabread

Makes 1
2 lb
loaf

Made with freshly harvested hedgerow berries, this tea loaf from Trelissick in Cornwall makes a delicious change from more traditional fruited breads. The garden here was created by Ronald Copeland who was chairman, and later managing director, of the Spode china factory. Many of the flowers that flourish in the mild Cornish air were the inspiration for the floral designs produced at the works.

2⅓ cups all-purpose flour, sifted
1 tsp mixed spice
1½ sticks butter, softened
¾ cup superfine sugar
8 oz fresh or frozen blackberries (if frozen, use straight from the freezer)
Grated rind and juice of 1 lemon
1 tbsp molasses
2 eggs, beaten
½ tsp baking soda
2 tbsp milk

1   Preheat the oven to 350°F. Grease and line a 2 lb loaf pan. Mix together the flour and mixed spice and rub in the butter until the mixture bears a resemblance to fine breadcrumbs.

2   Add the sugar, blackberries, lemon rind and juice, molasses/treacle and eggs and mix well. Dissolve the baking soda in the milk, add to the mixture and beat well.

3   Pour into the prepared pan, smooth and bake for 45 minutes. Reduce the oven temperature to 300°F and cook for a further 30–45 minutes until a skewer comes out clean. Remove from the oven and leave in the pan for about 15 minutes before turning out onto a wire rack to cool.

This unusual loaf is an ideal and novel way of using the blackberries that flourish in our hedgerows every summer.

Barm Brack

Makes 1
2 lb
loaf

Another good example of the use of succulent dried fruits and candied peel to make a plain cake more interesting. Barm means "leaven" or "yeast" and Brack means speckled and refers to the fruit scattered through the dough. It was often made in flattened circles and is served sliced, sometimes toasted and spread with plenty of butter. At Halloween, a small coin, pea, ring or stick was concealed in the dough to predict the fortune of the person who found it—the coin meant riches, the pea meant no marriage, the ring foretold a wedding and the stick indicated an unhappy marriage!

¾ cup currants
⅔ cup golden raisins
⅔ cup raisins
⅓ cup mixed candied peel
⅓ cup candied cherries, quartered
1 cup light soft brown sugar
1¼ cups cold black tea
Grated rind of 1 lemon
2 eggs, beaten
1¾ cups self-rising flour, sifted
1 tsp mixed spice
Pinch of salt

1 Put the dried fruit and candied cherries into a bowl with the sugar, tea and lemon rind and leave to soak for at least 3 hours, preferably longer.

2 Preheat the oven to 350°F. Grease and line a 2 lb loaf pan. Add the eggs, flour, mixed spice and salt to the fruit mixture and mix thoroughly.

3 Turn into the prepared pan and bake for 1½–1¾ hours until a skewer comes out clean. Remove from the oven and turn out onto a wire rack to cool. Serve sliced with butter.

Chelsea Buns

London's Chelsea Buns were originally made and sold in the Old Chelsea Bun House, a bakery owned and run in Pimlico, London, by Richard Hand, who was known by most people as Captain Bun.

1²/₃ cups white bread flour, sifted
½ oz fresh yeast (to substitute dried yeast, see page 36)
1 tsp superfine sugar
½ cup warm milk
½ oz shortening, e.g. Crisco, softened
Pinch of salt
1 egg, beaten
½ stick butter, melted
¹/₃ cup raisins
¹/₃ cup currants
¹/₃ cup golden raisins
¼ cup mixed candied peel
¹/₃ cup light soft brown sugar
Honey for glazing

1   Grease a 7 in square pan. Put ²/₃ cup of the flour into a bowl and add the yeast, superfine sugar and milk. Mix to a smooth batter and leave in a warm place for 20 minutes until frothy.

2   Rub the shortening into the remaining flour. Add the salt, the yeast mixture and the beaten egg, and mix to a soft dough. Knead on a floured board for about 5 minutes until really smooth. Place in a bowl, cover with a clean, damp cloth and leave in a warm place for 1–1½ hours until doubled in size.

3   Knead the dough again on a floured board and then roll out to a rectangle 9 x 12 in. Brush the melted butter over the surface and sprinkle the dried fruit and brown sugar over, leaving a narrow border all the way round the edge. Roll up like a jellyroll, starting with the longer side. Brush the edges of the dough with water and seal.

4   Cut the roll into nine pieces and place the rolls, cut side uppermost, in the prepared pan. Leave in a warm place for a further 30 minutes until well risen.

5   Meanwhile, preheat the oven to 375°F. When the buns are risen, bake for 30–35 minutes until golden. Remove from the oven, turn out on to a wire rack and, while still warm, brush the tops with honey. To serve, pull apart and eat warm or cold.

Marmalade & Apricot Teabread

Makes 1
1 lb
loaf

When in need of a snack to keep him going, my Dad used to wander around the house clutching a marmalade sandwich. This teabread is dedicated to him. If he were still here, he'd probably enjoy it, but I do acknowledge that he'd secretly be hankering after the white bread and thick-cut marmalade approach.

Scant 1½ cups all-purpose flour
2 tsp ground ginger
1 tsp baking powder
Scant ½ stick unsalted butter
¼ cup dark brown sugar
Scant ⅔ cup chopped ready-to-eat dried apricots
4 tbsp marmalade
Scant ⅓ cup milk
1 large free-range egg, beaten

1   Preheat the oven to 325°F. Grease and line a 1 lb loaf pan. Sift the flour, ginger and baking powder into a large bowl and rub in the butter until the mixture looks like breadcrumbs. Then stir in the sugar and the chopped apricots.

2   In another bowl, or a jug, mix up the marmalade, milk and egg and pour that onto the dry mixture. Mix it all up really well and pour it into the pan. Level the top and bake for about 1 hour, or until golden, firm to the touch and a skewer comes out cleanly. Turn the loaf onto a wire rack to cool.

3   I sometimes make some candied orange peel to go on top, but this is entirely optional. All you need to do is pare some strips of orange peel and put them into a pan with about ⅔ cup water and 3 tbsp superfine sugar. Bring the pan to a boil and then slowly simmer for about an hour or until the peel has gone translucent and the liquid has reduced by about half. Don't let the liquid reduce to a caramel or you will end up with something else altogether! Remove the orange strips from the pan and leave on silicone paper to cool and dry. Sprinkle with more superfine sugar if you wish.

Gently Spiced Fruit Loaf

Makes 1 large loaf that will serve 8 hungry people

This is the sort of fruity bread that makes people whimper slightly. It has everything: warm spices, gorgeous fruit, soft bread and a drizzle of lemony frosting. Ooooh. Yes, please. You decide what fruit to use—it's all good.

For the dough:
Scant ½ stick unsalted butter
2 cups white bread flour
Scant ¼ cup superfine sugar
A pinch of salt
¼ oz sachet dried yeast
Scant ½ cup hand-hot milk
3 large free-range egg yolks

For the filling:
2 cups water
2 cups dried fruit (apricots, cranberries, dates, figs, peaches, etc.), chopped
Zest and juice of 1 large unwaxed lemon
Zest and juice of 1 large orange
2 tbsp runny honey
1 tsp ground coriander
1 tsp cardamom seeds, crushed

For the frosting:
Scant ¾ cup confectioners' sugar, sifted
Juice of 1 large lemon
Slivered/flaked almonds to sprinkle (optional)

1 Start by making the dough. In a large bowl, rub the butter into the flour until it resembles breadcrumbs and then stir in the sugar, salt and yeast. Pour in the hot milk and 2 egg yolks and mix to form a dough. Turn the dough out onto a floured surface and knead the dough until it's smooth and elastic—this will take at least 10 minutes. Put the dough back into the bowl and cover with a tea towel or a layer of plastic wrap and leave to rise somewhere warm for at least 1 hour. The dough should double in size.

2 While the dough is rising, make the filling. Put the water in a big pan and bring it to the boil. Add the chopped dried fruit and simmer, stirring every now and again until the fruit is really soft. Add the citrus zest and juice, honey and spices and continue bubbling gently until the liquid has been absorbed by the fruit. Stir it every so often as it can catch on the bottom of the pan if left alone too long. Leave the mixture to cool down.

3 When the dough has doubled in size and the fruity filling is cool, take the dough out of the bowl and give it 2–3 bashes to knock the air out of it. Knead it again for another 3–4 minutes, then roll it out into a large rectangle about ½ in thick. Spread the fruit over the surface, leaving a gap around the edge of about ¾ in. Roll up the dough as you would a jellyroll and press the edges together to seal, then coil it around so you end up with a circular sausage. Place it on a baking sheet with the seal underneath. Pop the tea towel over the top again and leave it in the warm place for another hour to rise.

4 Preheat the oven to 350°F and, just before the loaf goes in the oven, brush it all over with the remaining egg yolk. Bake for about 20 minutes. It will be done when it is risen and golden on the top and the bottom sounds hollow when you give it a knock. Cool the loaf on a wire rack and make a very thin frosting with the confectioners' sugar and lemon juice. When cool, randomly drizzle the frosting over the top of the loaf and sprinkle the almonds on top, if liked.

Apple & Walnut Teabread

Makes 1
1½ lb
loaf

This teabread has to be one of the most versatile numbers going. Make it sweet, make it savory, make it big, make it small—it really is a wonder. Just delicious with a lump of strong Cheddar, or equally good with a smear of butter and a cup of tea—even au naturel, packed in a lunch box. It's easy to make and keeps well for ages in an airtight container. Surely this recipe must belong to a "hero" category?

Scant 1 stick unsalted butter
Scant ½ cup superfine sugar
2 large free-range eggs
1 tbsp corn syrup
²/₃ cup golden raisins
¾ cup chopped walnuts
1²/₃ cups self-rising flour
1 tsp mixed spice
1 tsp ground cinnamon
2 dessert apples, peeled, cored and chopped

1 Preheat the oven to 325°F. Grease and line a 1½ lb loaf pan or lay out 12 mini loaf cases on a baking sheet. Put all the ingredients into a big bowl and give them a bit of a beating. I put them in the mixer because I'm lazy, but a wooden spoon would be just as good. Don't use a food processor, though, because you will pulverize the apple too much.

2 Tip the lot into the loaf pan or mini loaf cases and bake the biggie for about 1 hour or the littlies for about 20 minutes. A knife or skewer will come out cleanly when they are cooked. Cool the big one on a wire rack and leave the little ones to cool in their cases.

Ultimate Loaf Cakes

Cakes cooked in a loaf pan (or tin, as they are called in Britain) are a British teatime staple—serve as elegant slices on dainty plates for a sophisticated Afternoon Tea, with butter on the side for extra indulgence.

Fig & raisin teabread
Makes one 2 lb loaf

I don't think we generally cook enough with dried figs. I adore them and encourage you to use them at every opportunity. Naturally sweet, soft, yet slightly crunchy from the seeds and really, really good for you. Yum.

1⅔ cups all-purpose flour
Scant 1 stick unsalted butter
½ cup dried figs, chopped
½ cup demerara sugar
Scant ½ cup chopped pecan nuts (optional)
Scant ⅔ cup raisins
1 tsp baking powder
1 tsp baking soda
⅔ cup milk

1 Preheat the oven to 325°F. Grease and line a 2 lb loaf pan. Put the flour into a large bowl and rub the butter into it until the mixture looks like breadcrumbs. Stir in the figs, sugar, pecan nuts (if you are using them) and raisins.

2 Mix the baking powder, baking soda and milk together and pour into the dry mix. Mix really well, adding a drop more milk if you need to, so that you have a good dropping consistency. Tip the batter into the pan and bake for about 1 hour or until firm to the touch and a knife or skewer comes out cleanly. Cool the loaf on a wire rack.

Malt loaf
Makes one 1 lb loaf

I remember that after number one son was born the midwife told me that malt loaf was an ideal snack for breastfeeding women—full of energy-giving properties, packed with vitamins, easy to eat one-handed and really a bit of a superfood. I took her advice very seriously and consumed absolutely gargantuan quantities of it. It was just the excuse I was looking for. It was quite a while before I could face any again. However, those days are long gone and I happily tuck in to malt loaf with the same gusto as all those years ago. Malt extract is available in wholefood stores.

⅔ cup raisins
⅔ cup golden raisins
Scant ½ stick unsalted butter
⅔ cup water
1¼ cups self-rising flour
½ tsp baking soda
A pinch of salt
⅔ cup dark dark brown sugar
1 large free-range egg, beaten
1 tbsp malt extract

1 Preheat the oven to 350°F. Grease and line a 1 lb loaf pan. Put the dried fruit, butter and water into a pan, bring to a boil, reduce the heat and simmer gently for 5 minutes. Let the mixture cool for a bit.

2 In a large bowl, mix together the flour, baking soda, salt and sugar. Stir in the wet mixture followed by the egg and the malt. Give everything a good stir.

3 Tip the batter into the pan and bake for about 1 hour or until a knife or skewer comes out clean. Cool in the pan, then slice, butter and tuck in.

Earl Grey loaf
Makes one 1½ lb loaf

If you don't like Earl Grey tea you could use another type—try Assam, Darjeeling or Lapsang Souchong. If push comes to shove, use builder's tea. And no, I haven't made a mistake—there isn't any fat in this one. Hurrah for that, and butter it at will.

1½ cups raisins or golden raisins
¾ cup strong cold Earl Grey tea
1⅔ cups self-rising flour
Generous ¾ cup demerara sugar
1 large free-range egg

1 Soak the raisins in the tea overnight. The next day, preheat the oven to 325°F and grease and line a 1½ lb loaf pan.

2 If you haven't been organized enough to soak your fruit, don't panic—put the raisins and the tea in a saucepan, bring to a boil, reduce the heat and simmer gently for 20 minutes. Not quite as good, but not bad.

3 Tip the fruit and remaining tea into a large bowl and simply stir in everything else. That's it. Tip the batter into the pan and bake for about 1 hour or until a knife or skewer comes out cleanly. Let the cake cool in the pan for 10 minutes before turning out onto a wire rack to cool completely.

Parkin
Serves 16

I always think of parkin as rather old-fashioned. In my book, old-fashioned combined with cake usually means extremely delicious. This is a real honest, no-frills bake and it's definitely, definitely best eaten a couple of days after you have made it. Accompanying cup of tea is non-negotiable.

1¼ cups all-purpose flour
4¼ cups medium oatmeal
1 tbsp dark brown sugar
1 tsp ground ginger
1 lb molasses
1 stick unsalted butter
Scant ⅓ cup milk
1 tsp baking soda

1 Preheat the oven to 350°F. Grease and line an 8 in square cake pan. Sift the flour into a large bowl, followed by the oatmeal, sugar and ginger.

2 In a pan, very gently heat the molasses and butter so that they melt, then remove from the heat. Warm the milk to hand-hot and add the baking soda. Then pour both the milk and the molasses and butter mixture into the dry ingredients and gently mix it all together. Don't go hell for leather here—a gentle approach is called for.

3 Tip the batter into the pan and bake for 40 minutes or until firm to the touch and a knife or skewer comes out clean. Cool on a wire rack before cutting into squares and storing in an airtight container for a few days before eating.

Date & walnut teabread
Makes one 2 lb loaf

Dates have a natural affinity with teabreads. Their sweetness and moistness adds not just flavor but the gorgeous texture that is called for here. Dates and walnuts, of course, are no strangers and so it is only right and proper that they appear together in a teabread.

½ cup unsalted butter
3 tbsp corn syrup
1 tbsp molasses
⅔ cup milk
2 large free-range eggs
1¾ cups whole-wheat all-purpose flour
1 tsp ground cinnamon
1 tsp baking soda
¾ cup chopped walnuts
1¼ cups stoned dates, chopped

1 Preheat the oven to 325°F. Grease and line a 2 lb loaf pan. Melt the butter, syrup and molasses together in a pan over a low heat until they are well amalgamated and then, off the heat, stir in the milk. Let the mixture cool a little then beat in the eggs (if you add them too soon you will end up with scrambled eggs).

2 Sift the dry ingredients into a large bowl (I use the freestanding mixer) and then beat in the syrup mixture. Fold in the walnuts and dates, tip the batter into the pan and bake for about 1½ hours. It is done when a knife or skewer comes out clean. Cool in the pan.

Lavender teabread
Makes one 1½ lb loaf

Lavender in a cake isn't as mad as you might think. It's definitely a summery number and goes well with a dollop of mascarpone cheese and some juicy fresh strawberries. Use lavender that you know hasn't been sprayed with nasty chemicals or by your neighbor's cat. and give it a good wash before you use it.

3 tbsp lavender flowers
¾ cup milk
1½ sticks unsalted butter
¾ cup superfine sugar
2 large free-range eggs, beaten
2⅓ cups all-purpose flour
A pinch of salt
1 tsp baking powder

1 Preheat the oven to 325°F. Grease and line a 1½ lb loaf pan. Put the lavender flowers in a small pan with the milk. Gently heat the milk until it barely reaches a simmer, then remove from the heat and let the lavender infuse in the milk for 20 minutes or so.

2 In a big bowl, cream the butter and sugar until pale and fluffy and then beat in the eggs slowly. Sift half the flour over the mixture together with the salt and baking powder and fold this in. Then carefully fold in half the milk and lavender mixture. Follow this with the second half of the flour and, finally, the remaining milk.

3 Pour the batter into the pan and bake for about 50 minutes or until a knife or skewer comes out clean. Cool in the pan for about 10 minutes before turning onto a wire rack.

If you can't find lavender, but want something similar, this recipe also works well with other fragrant herbs such as rosemary or lemon balm. As with the lavender, make sure the herbs haven't been sprayed with any chemicals and give them a good wash before you use them in your cake.

Lardy cake
Serves 8

Right, let's get this out of the way: this is possibly the most unhealthy, artery-clogging cake you will ever come across. It is also part of Britain's heritage and has been around for years and years because it is so amazingly delicious. It is filling, sweet, doughy, chewy and comforting.

1 oz fresh yeast, or ¾ oz dried yeast
1¼ cups warm water
1 tsp superfine sugar
3¼ cups white bread flour
2 tsp salt
¾ cup shortening, e.g. Crisco, chilled
½ cup currants
⅓ cup golden raisins
⅓ cup raisins
¾ cup superfine sugar

1 Grease a pan measuring about 8 x 10 in. Crumble the fresh (or dried) yeast over the warm water and add the 1 tsp of sugar. Blend it all so that the yeast dissolves, and set to one side for 15 minutes.

2 Put the flour and salt into a large bowl and add just 1 tbsp of the shortening. Rub the shortening into the flour and then add the yeast liquid. Mix it all up so that it forms a dough.

3 Turn the dough out onto a floured surface and knead for about 10 minutes or until it is smooth and elastic. Put the dough back in the bowl, cover with plastic wrap and leave somewhere warm for 30 minutes to rise.

4 Take the dough out of the bowl, knock out the air and roll it into a rectangle about ¼ in thick. Cut the remaining shortening into little cubes and sprinkle a third of it over the dough, followed by a third of the fruit and a third of the sugar.

5 Fold the bottom third of the dough upwards and the top third of the dough downwards and give the whole thing a half turn so you have a vertical rectangle in front of you. Roll this out until you get to a rectangle and repeat the whole process. Then do it again. Once you have incorporated all the shortening, sugar and fruit and done the final bit of folding, roll the dough to fit the pan and carefully put it in. Stab it 6–8 times right the way through the dough. Cover with a tea towel and leave to prove in a warm place for 30 minutes.

6 Preheat the oven to 425°F. Score the top of the cake into 8, if you like, and bake for about 45 minutes or until golden brown. Cool in the pan. If it's difficult to turn out because of all the sticky loveliness in the bottom of the pan, give it a bit of heat and it will release. Smear all the goo back over the lardy.

Bara brith
Serves 10

This is a traditional Welsh teabread, the name of which translates as "speckled bread". There are many versions of this delicious loaf—some use yeast, others self-rising flour. I've gone for the self-rising flour option for the sole reason that it keeps much better. The version made with yeast needs eating that day. This one is simplicity itself and really calls for a good slathering of butter.

2⅔ cups mixed dried fruit
1⅓ cups tea
2 tbsp marmalade
1 large free-range egg, beaten
6 tbsp dark brown sugar
1 tsp mixed spice
3¼ cups self-rising flour
2 tbsp runny honey for glazing

1 Soak the fruit overnight in the tea. Next day, preheat the oven to 325°F and grease and line a 1½ lb loaf pan.

2 Mix everything apart from the honey in a large bowl and, when it is thoroughly mixed, tip it into the loaf pan. Level the top and bake for about 1½ hours. You may need to protect the top of the loaf with parchment paper if it looks as if it is over-browning. It is done when a knife or skewer comes out clean.

3 While the cake is warm, tip it onto a wire rack and brush the top with the runny honey. Leave to cool completely before cutting.

Bite-sized Treats

English Madeleines

Makes 8 in pudding basins (probably 10 in dariole molds)

I say "English" because they really couldn't be more different from their better-known French counterparts. I make these when I need a blitz of borderline comedy in the cake department. They are ridiculous, if we are honest, but do taste good, which is the important thing. You are meant to use dariole molds to get the right shape but I use little pudding basins that make them look even more ridiculous.

Scant ½ cup unsalted butter
Scant ½ cup superfine sugar
2 large free-range eggs, lightly beaten
Scant ¾ cup self-rising flour, sifted
3 tbsp strawberry jam, sieved
Scant 1 cup desiccated coconut
8–10 candied cherries

1 Preheat the oven to 325°F and grease your chosen molds. I like to line the base with a disc of parchment paper too, just to be on the safe side.

2 Beat the butter and the sugar together until really pale and fluffy and slowly beat in the eggs, a little at a time. Then fold in the flour. Spoon the batter into the molds and bake for about 20 minutes, or until springy and firm to the touch. Leave them in their molds for 5 minutes before turning them out onto a wire rack to cool. If they're being stubborn, run a knife along the edge of the molds and give them a good sharp tap on the bottom.

3 When the cakes are properly cold, slice off the tops so that they have a very flat base when you turn them upside down. Brush the jam over the whole of each cake and cover in the coconut. I favor the throw-it-on approach; I put the coconut in a deep, wide dish, place the cakes on top of the coconut and sling small handfuls of coconut at the side and the top. Top with a cherry.

Macarons

Makes about 20 (10 with filling)

Macarons make me smile. I love their garish colors, their unusual flavors, their crisp outer and squidgy inner. I also love the fact that they're gone in two mouthfuls, so you can legitimately have quite a few without looking excessively greedy. I've given you the basic version here, and it's up to you to add whatever flavors take your fancy. I make them with rosewater, lavender, lime, mandarin, lemon and bergamot.

1¼ cups confectioners' sugar
1¼ cups ground almonds
3 large free-range egg whites
⅓ cup superfine sugar
Food coloring (optional)
2–3 drops of flavoring (optional)
Scant ¾ stick unsalted butter, softened
1⅓ cups confectioners' sugar, sifted

1   Preheat the oven to 325°F and line two baking sheets with silicone liners. In a food processor, blitz the confectioners' sugar and the ground almonds. I know they are already ground, but this extra milling makes all the difference. Then sieve the mixture into a large bowl. Discard any chunky bits that remain in the sieve.

2   In another bowl, whisk the egg whites until really stiff and then whisk in the superfine sugar until you have a glossy meringue. Add the food coloring and the flavoring to the meringue and continue to whisk.

3   Then, very carefully (I do this in three goes), fold the meringue into the dry ingredients and continue folding until the mixture leaves a ribbon trail. Carefully spoon the mixture into a decorating bag fitted with a plain tube and pipe small blobs (about 1 in across) onto the sheets, leaving a good gap between each macaron.

4   Next is the crucial bit. It's not often I get really strict, but listen up: leave the macarons to dry out in the air until they form a skin. Do not, do you hear me, attempt to bake them while they are tacky to the touch. This may take 10 minutes, it may take 45. It really does depend on the humidity of the surroundings.

5   Have they formed a skin? Yes? Good, let's move on. Pop them in the oven for 15 minutes or so. They're done when you can gently prod them along the liner. Not budging? Probably not done yet. When you're happy, take them out and carefully put them on a wire rack to cool.

6   Make the buttercream filling by beating the butter and the confectioners' sugar together. Add color and flavor to match the macarons and, when they are cool, sandwich them together, pile them up and marvel at your brilliance.

Eccles Cakes

I love the thought of Eccles cakes, but whenever I eat them I realize why I don't have them more often: chopped mixed peel. Bleuch. I can't stand the stuff. It makes me shudder just to think about it, sitting there all orange and yellow in its little round tub, just waiting to make you contort your face in disgust. I made Eccles cakes with just currants. They were lovely. Someone should make it the law. Much nicer.

1 x 18 oz packet all-butter puff pastry (to make your own see page 58)
¼ stick very soft unsalted butter
½ cup currants
2 tbsp dark brown sugar
Finely grated zest of 1 unwaxed lemon
Finely grated zest of 1 orange
1–2 drops of lemon oil (optional)
Superfine sugar for sprinkling

1 Preheat the oven to 425°F. Roll out the pastry to about ⅛ in thick and cut out 10 circles (more if you can).

2 In a bowl, mix the butter, currants, sugar and fruit zests. I sometimes add a drop or two of lemon oil to the proceedings. Place a tsp of the mixture into the very center of each pastry circle. Bundle up the outer edges as if to make a purse and squidge the edges together to seal the little parcel.

3 Turn each parcel over, seal-side down, and roll it out into a flatter circle so that the currants just start to peek through. Prick all over with a fork and place on the baking sheet. Bake for about 15 minutes or until golden brown. When they are out of the oven, transfer to a wire rack and sprinkle with superfine sugar while they are still warm.

If you are a fan of mixed peel try adding a tablespoon to the currant mixture for a more traditional version of the recipe.

Apple Muffins with Cinnamon Butter

Throw together a batch of these comforting muffins and find your kitchen filled with the sweet smell of cinnamon. For a fuss-free but to-die-for twist, serve them still warm, broken open and smeared with melting cinnamon butter.

2 cups self-rising flour
½ tsp baking soda
1 tsp ground cinnamon
2 eggs, beaten
Scant ⅓ cup plain yogurt
Scant ½ cup milk
⅔ cup soft brown sugar
6 tbsp sunflower oil
2 apples, peeled, cored and finely diced

For the cinnamon butter
1 stick butter, at room temperature
½ cup confectioners' sugar, sifted
1 tsp ground cinnamon

1 Preheat the oven to 400°F. Grease or line a 12-hole muffin pan.

2 Combine the flour, baking soda and cinnamon and sift into a large bowl.

3 In a separate bowl, combine the eggs, yogurt, milk, brown sugar and oil, then stir in the apples. Pour the mixture into the dry ingredients and stir together until just combined, then spoon big dollops of the batter into the prepared muffin pan.

4 Bake for about 20 minutes until risen and golden. Leave to cool in the pan for a couple of minutes, then transfer to a wire rack to cool.

5 Meanwhile, beat together the butter, confectioners' sugar and cinnamon. Serve the muffins warm, with the cinnamon butter for spreading.

Lemon & Almond Crumbles

Lemony, almondy, moist, moreish ... what's not to like? These are another of those easy muffins that somehow elicit an air of sophistication and make you feel rather ladylike—until you find yourself trying to resist the urge to eat more than one!

1²/₃ cups self-rising flour
1 tsp baking powder
Scant ²/₃ cup superfine sugar
Generous 1 cup ground almonds
1 egg, beaten
1 cup milk
Scant ½ cup butter, melted
grated zest of 2 lemons
½ cup slivered/flaked almonds for sprinkling
Confectioners' sugar for dusting

1 Preheat the oven to 400°F. Grease or line a 12-hole muffin pan.

2 Combine the flour, baking powder and superfine sugar and sift into a large bowl. Sprinkle the ground almonds into the bowl.

3 In a separate bowl or jug, combine the egg, milk, butter and lemon zest, then pour into the dry ingredients. Stir together until just combined, then spoon big dollops of the batter into the prepared muffin pan. Sprinkle the tops with the slivered/flaked almonds.

4 Bake for about 20 minutes until risen and golden. Leave to cool in the pan for a few minutes, then transfer to a wire rack to cool. Serve dusted with confectioners' sugar.

These dainty muffins are even cuter if you make them in a mini muffin pan— but be sure to reduce the baking time .

Espresso Express

Make these in the morning when you need a bit of jet-fuel to get you going. After munching your way through the coffee-flavored crumb specked with whole chocolate-covered coffee beans and all topped off with a lusciously creamy, sugary coffee buttercream, nothing's going to stop you!

2 cups all-purpose flour
1 tbsp baking powder
Scant ⅔ cup superfine sugar
¼ cup chocolate-covered coffee beans
1 egg, beaten
¾ cup milk
2 tbsp Greek yogurt
2 tbsp instant coffee, dissolved in 2 tbsp boiling water
¾ stick butter, melted

For the topping
Scant 1 stick butter, at room temperature
1¾ cups confectioners' sugar, sifted
2 tsp instant coffee, dissolved in 1 tbsp boiling water
Chocolate-covered coffee beans to decorate

1 Preheat the oven to 400°F. Grease or line a 12-hole muffin pan.

2 Combine the flour, baking powder and superfine sugar and sift into a large bowl, then scatter the coffee beans on top.

3 In a separate bowl or jug, lightly beat together the egg, milk, yogurt and coffee, then stir in the melted butter. Pour into the dry ingredients and stir together until just combined, then spoon big dollops of the batter into the prepared muffin pan.

4 Bake for about 20 minutes until risen and firm to the touch. Leave to cool in the pan for a few minutes, then transfer the muffins to a wire rack to cool completely.

5 To decorate, beat together the butter, confectioners' sugar and coffee until smooth and creamy. Swirl on top of the muffins and decorate with more chocolate-covered coffee beans.

Peppermint Stick Muffins

Let the kids help you make these magnificently minty muffins. They'll love bashing the mints to break them up, and save you a lot of energy! Look out for stripy sticks of rock or candy cane and tint the frosting in a contrasting color to really make them stand out.

2 cups self-rising flour
1 tsp baking powder
Generous ⅓ cup superfine sugar
2 packets of extra strong mints
(1½ oz each)
2 eggs, beaten
1 cup milk
Scant ½ cup butter, melted

To decorate
3 sticks of peppermint candy cane
(about 3 oz)
1¾ cups confectioners' sugar, sifted
2 tbsp lemon juice
Food coloring (optional)

1 Preheat the oven to 400°F. Grease or line a 12-hole muffin pan.

2 Combine the flour, baking powder and superfine sugar, then sift into a bowl. Put the mints in a mortar and pound with a pestle to break them up into small pieces. Scatter them over the flour.

3 In a separate bowl or jug, lightly beat together the eggs and milk to combine, then stir in the butter. Pour into the dry ingredients and stir together until just combined, then spoon dollops of the batter into the prepared muffin pan.

4 Bake for about 20 minutes until risen and golden. Leave to cool in the pan for a few minutes, then transfer to a wire rack to cool.

5 To decorate, put the candy cane or rock in a plastic bag and tap with a rolling pin to break into pieces. Set aside. Stir together the confectioners' sugar and lemon juice until smooth, then add a few drops of food coloring to tint the frosting, if you like. Spoon on top of the muffins and sprinkle pieces of candy cane or rock on top.

Carrot Cupcakes with Honey Orange Frosting

There are so many recipes for carrot cake around that I'd say, if you have a favorite one, try it in cupcake liners. This is my favorite—one of those recipes on a scrappy bit of paper tucked into my collection. I like the fact that the frosting contains no sugar, being sweetened with honey. One thing I would suggest—use only proper cream cheese—sometimes sold as curd cheese. I've never had much success with the white soft cheese sold in supermarkets everywhere. It's too runny.

Generous ¾ cup soft brown sugar
¾ cup sunflower oil
3 large free-range eggs
1 cup all-purpose flour
1½ tsp baking soda
1½ tsp baking powder
1 tsp ground cinnamon
½ tsp freshly grated nutmeg
A pinch of salt
2 cups grated or shredded carrot

For the cream cheese frosting
1 x 8 oz packet curd/cream cheese
(not soft or light cream cheese),
softened
2 tsp honey (or more to taste)
Grated zest of 1 unwaxed orange
Orange sprinkles to decorate

1 Preheat the oven to 350°F. Line a 12-hole muffin pan with cupcake liners. Mix the sugar and oil in a large bowl. Add the eggs and mix well. Sift in the dry ingredients, and beat everything together until really well combined. Next add the grated carrots and stir through well.

2 Place spoonfuls of batter in the prepared cases, and bake in the oven for 15–20 minutes. Watch these like a hawk, as they have a tendency to burn. If the tops are getting a bit dark and it looks like the innards are still raw, cover with parchment paper, and cook a little longer. Remove from the oven and leave to cool.

3 While they are cooling, make the frosting. Put the cream cheese in a bowl, and beat until softened. Stir in the honey and orange zest. Give it a taste to make sure it is sweet enough. Add a bit more honey if you want. When the cakes are cold, spread the frosting over the top and decorate at will.

Battenburg Cupcakes

I love the color combination of Battenburg and toyed with the idea of wrapping the whole caboodle in marzipan, but I settled on this version. I like the tang of the apricot jam, but you could use any other flavor. You don't have to stick to pink sponge, either. Why not green and blue?

1²/₃ cups self-rising flour
1 cup superfine sugar
1 cup margarine, softened
2 tsp baking powder
4 large free-range eggs
2 tsp pure vanilla extract
Pink food coloring (preferably gel)
Apricot jam for spreading
1 quantity lemon glacé frosting (see page 32)
Dolly mixture or other sprinkles to decorate

1 Preheat oven to 325°F. Grease two 8 in square cake pans, and line with baking parchment.

2 Sift the flour and sugar into a mixing bowl, food processor or food mixer. Add the margarine, baking powder, eggs and vanilla. Beat until light and fluffy. Divide the batter into two equal portions in separate bowls, and add a little bit of pink food coloring to one half. Pour each cake batter into a separate tin, and bake in the oven for 20–25 minutes until firm to the touch and golden. Don't worry that the pink cake doesn't look very pink. Remove from the oven and turn both cakes onto wire racks to cool.

3 Using a sharp knife, level the tops of the cakes so that the top and the bottom are completely flat. Spread a thin layer of apricot jam over the upper side of the pink layer. Place the plain cake on top so that the bottom side of the sponge faces upwards. Cut into ¾ in strips.

4 Now, pay attention. Lay one strip on its side so that you have a line of pink and a line of yellow. Spread a thin layer of jam over the top. Take another strip of cake and lay it on its side on top of the jam strip, but reversed so that yellow lies directly on top of pink and vice versa. Cut these strips into squares, and drizzle with the glacé frosting. Let some of the frosting dribble down the sides. Plop a dolly mixture (or alternative adornment) on top, and place in cupcake liners.

Mini Cherry Tarts

Makes about 12

Yes, yes, this is my version of the cherry Bakewell tart, one of my all-time favorite cakes. But, get this—no fat, no flour and contains fruit and nuts. Not only is it perfectly wonderful for gluten-intolerant personages, but also it must somehow count as "good for you". Surely?

4 large free-range eggs, separated
¾ cup superfine sugar
2¼ cups ground almonds
1 tsp baking powder (or ½ tsp baking soda and 1 tsp cream of tartar if you want to keep it gluten-free)
12 candied cherries

For the decoration
1 quantity lemon glacé frosting (see page 32)
Golf-ball-sized piece of rolled fondant
Red food coloring (preferably gel)
edible glue
Red edible glitter
Green food coloring (preferably gel)
1 tbsp royal icing (see page 33)
Parchment decorating bag

1 Preheat the oven to 400°F. Line a 12-hole muffin pan with cupcake liners.

2 Beat the egg yolks and sugar together until pale. In a clean, dry separate bowl, whisk the egg whites until stiff peaks form. Gently fold them into the egg yolk mixture, then fold in the ground almonds and baking powder. Spoon the batter into the prepared cases, and push 1 cherry down into each sponge. Bake in the oven for 15–20 minutes, keeping an eye on them throughout—burnt almond doesn't taste good. Remove from the oven and leave to cool.

3 Make a glacé frosting (page 32) and pour a little over each cake. While you are waiting for the frosting to set (30 minutes), make the rolled fondant cherries. Dye the sugar paste red by dipping a toothpick/cocktail stick into the red food coloring and transferring it to the paste. Knead the color in evenly, then make little cherry-sized balls (one for each cupcake), paint them with the edible glue and roll them in the edible glitter.

4 When the frosting is dry, add a little food coloring to the royal icing to make it green. Fill a parchment decorating bag with the royal icing, squeezing down to the end. Snip the very end off the bag. Stick a sugar paste cherry onto each cupcake with a tiny blob of edible glue, and pipe stalks and leaves with the green royal icing.

Ultimate Cupcakes

Who needs an excuse to bake something scrumptious?
Whether it's Valentine's Day, Mother's Day or a Batchelorette party,
cupcakes can be dressed up for any special occasion.

Cupcake base recipe
Makes 12

Generous ¾ cup self-rising flour, sifted
½ cup superfine sugar, sifted
½ cup margarine, softened
1 tsp baking powder
2 large free-range eggs
1 tsp pure vanilla extract

1 Preheat the oven to 325°F. Line a 12-hole muffin pan with baking cups. Put all the ingredients in a mixer (food processor, food mixer, or just a big bowl with an electric whisk).

2 Mix really well until the batter is light and fluffy. Put heaped teaspoons of the batter into the prepared cases, and bake in the oven for about 20 minutes until golden, and firm and springy when you give them a light prod on top. Let them cool before preparing the frosting—on a wire rack if you want, but not 100 percent necessary.

English summer cupcakes
Makes 12

This recipe works really well as a dessert after a lovely summery lunch. This is another of those recipes that can look very elegant, but is very easy.

1½ cups mascarpone cheese
Selection of soft ripe fruit such as blueberries, strawberries, raspberries, peaches and nectarines

1 Empty the tub of mascarpone cheese into a bowl and give it a bit of a beating, but don't add anything to it. Place a dollop of mascarpone on top of each of the cupcakes, and artfully arrange the fruit on and around the cakes.

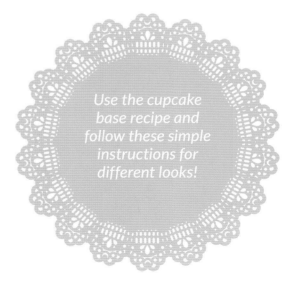

Use the cupcake base recipe and follow these simple instructions for different looks!

Mother's Day delights
Makes 12

You can buy pre-made sugar roses in most specialst cake decorating stores and on websites if you are pushed for time. Whatever you decide, these cupcakes will make a spectacular treat for Mother's Day.

1¾ cups confectioners' sugar, sifted
Boiling water
Gel food coloring
12 candied/sugared roses

1 To make the frosting, put the confectioners' sugar in a bowl, and slowly add boiling water until you have a thick soup consistency. Add the food coloring and pour over cakes. Wait about 10 minutes before carefully placing a rose on top of each cupcake.

Batchelorette party
Makes 12

These kinky cakes are guaranteed to get the party started. So let the fun begin, gals!

1 quantity of glacé frosting
(see page 32)
2 tbsp royal icing (see page 33)
Dark brown and pink gel food coloring

1 Ice your cooled cupcakes with pale pink glacé frosting. Leave to dry for at least 1 hour. Tint half the royal icing dark brown. If it gets too runny, add some more sifted confectioners' sugar. Put the brown royal icing in a decorating bag with a fine tube and the remaining white royal icing into another one.

2 With the brown royal icing, pipe 1950-style dresses onto a few cakes (small waists, big skirts), high heeled shoes on a few more and purses onto yet more. If you are stuck for ideas, look in a few magazines or draw out a few examples first. Fill in patterns and folds on the dresses, buckles and pockets on the bags, and stitch lines and other details on the shoes with the white royal icing. Make them as cheeky as you dare!

Easy-peasy heart cupcakes
Makes 12

Yes, there is some piping here. No, it isn't tricky. Royal icing is invaluable for piping. You can use it for frosting cakes if you like a very hard surface. What I suggest you do if you are a bit nervous about your piping skills is to practice on a plate or directly onto your work surface. When you are happy that you have the flow of the shape right, go for it! Let the base layer of frosting dry really well before you start decorating. If you want to create something other than hearts, do it. Tiny spots all over look really pretty and couldn't be simpler.

*1 quantity of cupcake base
(see page 166)
1 quantity of glacé frosting
(see page 32
2 tbsp royal icing (see page 33)
Food colorings (preferably gel)
Parchment decorating bag*

1 Make the cupcakes as for the recipe on page 166, and allow them to cool.

2 To make the glacé frosting, sift the confectioners' sugar into a bowl, and add the water drop by drop until you get the consistency you require (thick soup). Add the food coloring, and check that you still have the correct consistency—you may need to add a little more sifted confectioners' sugar. Spoon the frosting over the cakes and leave to dry. Leaving them for a couple of hours at this stage is really good, if you can.

3 Tint the royal icing with the food coloring, then use some to fill the parchment decorating bag, squeezing it down to the end.

4 Snip the very end off the bag. Practice piping the hearts or whatever shape you want, then pipe away to your heart's content on the top of each iced cupcake. Leave to dry for another hour or two before eating.

Gadzooks for the spooks
Makes 12

Black Halloween cupcakes are highly entertaining. Black frosting is wonderful—it transforms your teeth and mouth at first bite. There is absolutely no room for subtlety here. You can scare the living daylights out of trick-or-treaters, by having a mouthful of cake just before you open the door. Rest assured that the color does fade quite rapidly...

1 quantity of cupcake base (see page 166)
1 quantity of glacé frosting (see page 32)
Black and orange food coloring (preferably gel)
Golf ball-sized piece of rolled fondant
Edible glue
Small paintbrush

1 Make the cupcakes and allow to cool. Make up the glacé frosting, and divide into two portions; use the food coloring to make one black and the other deep orange. Divide the cupcakes into two batches, and ice one batch black and the other batch orange. Leave them to dry. (These cakes need to be completely dry before you add anything else because of the dark colors.)

2 Take a third of the rolled fondant and tint it black. Make a ghost by flattening out a piece of white sugar paste into the shape of a ghost and use edible glue to stick it onto a black-iced cupcake. Let the ghost trail over the edge of the cake in a ghostly manner. Take some tiny bits of black paste, and stick them on to make a ghoulish face for the ghost.

3 Make the spider by taking a bit of black paste the size of a fava/broad bean, and sticking it onto an orange-iced cake using edible glue. Make as many legs as you can (8 is traditional!) out of slivers of black paste, and stick them on. I also like to add a final strip of black for the web. A face and fangs made out of white rolled fondant finishes it off.

4 For the spooky eyes, take 2 elongated egg shapes of white rolled fondant, add black pupils and stick onto a black-iced cake.

Halloween super scaries
Makes 18–20

It's the time of year to roast some squash or pumpkin and then throw it into these irresistibly sweet and spicy little cakes. Look out for fake spiders and other nasties in kids' toy stores and hide a few on the plate to scare anyone else away ... leaving you with a big batch of cupcakes all to yourself!

7 oz peeled, seeded pumpkin, cut into chunks
½ tbsp sunflower oil
2 cups all-purpose flour
1 tbsp baking powder
1 tsp ground cinnamon
1 egg, beaten
Scant ⅔ cup sour cream
Scant/¼ cup milk
½ cup soft brown sugar
¼ cup butter, melted

To decorate
5 oz white chocolate
1 oz bittersweet chocolate

1 Preheat the oven to 375°F. Put the pumpkin in a baking dish, drizzle with the oil, then toss to coat. Roast for about 35 minutes until tender. Remove from the oven and leave to cool, then mash roughly with a fork.

2 To make the cupcakes, preheat the oven to 400°F. Line two 12-hole muffin pans with baking cups. Combine the flour, baking powder and cinnamon and sift into a large bowl. In a separate bowl, combine the egg, sour cream, milk, mashed squash, sugar and butter and stir together until well mixed. Pour into the dry ingredients and stir together until just combined, then spoon large dollops of the batter into the prepared muffin pan.

3 Bake for about 15 minutes until risen and golden. Leave to cool in the pan for a few minutes, then transfer to a wire rack.

4 To decorate, melt the white chocolate in a heatproof bowl set over a pan of barely simmering water, then spoon on top of the cakes. Melt the bittersweet chocolate in the same way in a separate bowl, then spoon into a decorating bag with a very narrow tube. Pipe concentric circles onto each cake, then use a skewer to draw a line from the center to the outside of each cake to make a spider's web pattern.

Easter muffins
Makes 12

When you're celebrating Easter with a gluten- or dairy-intolerant cake-eater, this is the recipe to choose. Inspired by the fruity marzipan simnel cake, these little muffins look cuter than cute topped off with baby chick yellow frosting and pastel-colored eggs. Be sure to check the ingredients on your pastel-colored eggs and marzipan to make sure they don't contain any dairy or gluten.

1½ cups potato flour
⅔ cup rice flour
1 tbsp cornstarch
1 tbsp gluten-free baking powder
Scant ½ cup superfine sugar
⅔ cup raisins or golden raisins
2 tbsp candied peel
1 egg, beaten
¾ cup soya milk
6 tbsp sunflower oil
3½ oz gluten-free marzipan, finely grated
Finely grated zest of 1 lemon

To decorate
1¾ cups confectioners' sugar, sifted
2 tbsp lemon juice
Yellow food coloring
Pastel-colored mini eggs

1 Preheat the oven to 400°F. Grease or line a 12-hole muffin pan.

2 Combine the flours, baking powder and superfine sugar and sift into a large bowl, then add the raisins or golden raisins and candied peel.

3 In a separate bowl or jug, combine the egg, milk and oil, then stir in the marzipan and lemon zest. Pour into the dry ingredients and stir together until just combined, then spoon large dollops of the batter into the prepared muffin pan.

4 Bake for about 20 minutes until risen and golden. Leave to cool in the pan for a few minutes, then transfer to a wire rack to cool.

5 To decorate, mix the confectioners' sugar and lemon juice until smooth, then add a few drops of food coloring to make a pale yellow frosting. Spoon on top of the cakes and top with mini eggs.

Fun for
Little Ones

Jam Doughnuts

I do not own a deep-fat fryer. If I did, I would want to fry absolutely everything, so it really is better if I don't have one to start with. The thought of having an open pan of boiling fat on the stove terrifies me. I would knock it over, or set the place on fire—and my hair would smell. So that's not happening. But I do love doughnuts. What to do, what to do? Bake them, that's what. These really taste like doughnuts and are almost good for you because they are baked not fried. Hurrah!

Scant 1½ cups white bread flour
¼ tsp salt
Scant 1 cup superfine sugar
Scant ¼ stick butter
¼ oz/7 g easy blend yeast
5 tbsp milk
1 large free-range egg, beaten
4 tbsp strawberry jam (or jam of your choice)
½ cup confectioners' sugar

1 Put the flour and salt and scant ¼ cup of the superfine sugar into a big bowl and rub in the butter until it looks like fine breadcrumbs, then stir in the yeast. Heat the milk until it is warm—so you can easily leave your finger in it without shrieking. Mix the milk and the egg into the flour mixture until it forms a dough. Flour a work surface (I like to have a pile of extra flour to one side, too) and tip the dough onto the work surface. Knead the dough until it stops being sticky (keep flouring your hands and adding a smidgen to the work surface) and keep going until the dough changes from being a bit rough under your fingers to beautifully smooth and elastic. Believe me, you'll know when you get there.

2 Put the dough back in the bowl and cover it with a tea towel. Leave in a warm place for about 1 hour or until doubled in size. Take the dough out and give it another knead for a couple

of minutes, then cut it into 12 equal pieces. Roll each ball out to a circle of about 4 in and put a smallish teaspoon of jam right in the middle. Gather up the edges of the circle around the jam and pinch it all together to make a seal. Place the filled doughnut seal-side down on a baking sheet and repeat the process, leaving lots of space between each one. Cover again with the tea towel and leave to rise for 45 minutes.

3 Preheat the oven to 350°F and bake the doughnuts for 10 minutes or until beautifully golden. Cool for a minute or so while you make the glaze. Mix the confectioners' sugar with enough water to make a thin, runny, frosting and brush each doughnut with it. Put the remaining superfine sugar in a deep dish and roll the doughnuts in it. Serve immediately.

Rock Buns

Ah, rock buns; the key element to any decent fête, school cake sale, or homemade cake competition. You really can't beat them. Rock-like in appearance, but not in texture, all hail the unsung hero of small cakes. Cup of tea obligatory and I like a whopper of a rock cake. A boulder, I suppose. So the numbers specified are entirely unreliable but based upon what I would sneeringly consider a "normal" size. Shudder.

1²/₃ cups all-purpose flour
2 tsp baking powder
1 stick unsalted butter
Scant ½ cup demerara sugar, plus 2 tbsp
Scant ½ cup mixed dried fruit
Grated zest of 1 unwaxed lemon
1 large free-range egg
1–2 tbsp milk

1 Preheat the oven to 350°F and grease and line two baking sheets. Sift the flour and baking powder into a bowl and then rub in the butter so that the mixture resembles breadcrumbs. Add the ½ cup demerara sugar, the mixed fruit and the lemon zest and give it a good old stir. Add the egg and 1 tbsp of the milk and mix until you have a stiff, but moist dough. Add the remaining milk if you need to.

2 Grab two forks and form rock-like shapes in heaps on the baking sheet—this is where you get to make stones, rocks or boulders. Sprinkle the 2 tbsp demerara sugar over the top of your buns and bake for about 20 minutes or until they are golden brown. Cool on a wire rack and serve

Play around with the sizes of these and see which you like best!

Fondant Fancies

Very few cakes get the consistent reaction that I get with these. And it's a good reaction. Make these and a Battenburg and grown men will weep at your feet.

¾ cup soft margarine
1¼ cups self-rising flour, sifted
¾ cup superfine sugar
3 large free-range eggs
1½ tsp vanilla extract
Scant ¾ stick unsalted butter, softened
3 cups confectioners' sugar, sifted
Food coloring

1   Preheat the oven to 325°F. Grease and line an 8½ in square cake pan. Put the margarine, flour, superfine sugar, eggs and 1 tbsp vanilla into a freestanding mixer and beat until the batter is light and fluffy. Pour it into the pan and bake for about 20 minutes or until firm and springy to the touch and a knife or skewer comes out cleanly. Cool the sponge on a wire rack.

2   Meanwhile, make the buttercream. Cream together the butter and 1⅓ cup confectioners' sugar with the remaining vanilla until really pale and creamy. You may need to add a drop of milk if the mixture is really stiff—you need to be able to pipe this stuff. Put the buttercream into a decorating bag fitted with a plain tube. Cut the cold cake into squares and pipe a small blob of buttercream into the center of each cake. Let the buttercream dry for a minute or two while you make the frosting.

3   Mix a small amount of water into the remaining confectioners' sugar until you have an frosting that thickly coats the back of a spoon. If it is too runny, add more confectioners' sugar; too thick, add a drop more water. Tint the frosting whatever color you like. Put the cakes on a wire rack over a tray and spoon the frosting over the top of each cake so that it runs down the sides. You may need to tease it over the corners, but let the frosting do the work for you. Leave to dry on their rack for an hour.

4   Make up a little more frosting if you wish and drizzle a contrasting zigzag line across each cake. You can do this directly off a spoon or with a decorating bag. Now, square baking cups don't appear to exist. Lay out the required number of round cupcake liners and open them out a bit. Place each cake in a case and wrap the edges of the cases round the cakes. If you do this while the frosting is slightly tacky, it will stick.

Cherry Buns

This was often made in the 1970s without the aid of a mixer. Just me, my wooden spoon and quite a lot of mess. I was utterly, utterly happy and all my thoughts about the lack of a Barbie pony in my life were forgotten because I was making cherry buns. I added the frosting because, in my grown-up world, I can. In the 1970s, they were naked, but this is the exact recipe I used.

⅓ cup margarine
⅓ cup superfine sugar
1 large free-range egg
Scant 1 cup self-rising flour
Grated zest of 1 unwaxed lemon
2 tbsp candied cherries, quartered
2–3 tbsp milk

1 Preheat the oven to 350°F. Line a 12-hole bun pan with baking cups

2 Cream the margarine and sugar, using a wooden spoon (it said so, so I did), until the mixture is light and creamy. Beat in the egg.

3 Sift the flour into a second bowl. Add the lemon zest and cherries to the flour and mix in. Add the flour to the creamed mixture and stir well so that all the ingredients are thoroughly mixed.

4 Add enough milk to make the batter just soft enough to drop from the spoon. Put a big teaspoonful into each baking cup and bake for 20–25 minutes.

These jaunty little buns look great in patterned cases!

Gingerbread Gangland

This dough is very easy to make and you don't end up with those hard-as-stone cookies. I implore you to go to town with the decoration. There is room for some minor acts of subversion here—I like to turn the gingerbread boys and girls into really naughty people, sticking their tongues out and forgetting to put their trousers on. Shun the world of currant buttons, embrace the decorating bag and take the road to gingerbread badness...

2 ⅓ cups all-purpose flour (but you may need more)
1 tsp baking soda
2 tsp ground ginger
1 stick butter
scant 1 cup soft light brown sugar
1 large free-range egg
4 tbsp corn syrup
4 tbsp royal icing (see page 33)
Food coloring gels
Silver dragées
Several parchment paper decorating bags and size 2 tubes

1   Sift the flour, baking soda and ginger into a large bowl. Add the butter and rub it in with your fingertips until you have a mixture resembling fine breadcrumbs. Add the sugar and give it a good mix.

2   In another bowl, beat the egg and corn syrup together. I find a whisk works wonders here. Tip it over the flour mix and stir well. You may find it easier to get your hands in at this point. Sometimes the dough can be a bit on the sticky side. Keep sprinkling over flour and working it in until you have a lovely smooth dough.

3   Wrap the dough in plastic wrap and leave to chill in the refrigerator for at least 30 minutes, but an hour would be better.

4   Preheat the oven to 375°F and line two baking sheets with silicone liners.

5   Roll the dough out on a lightly floured surface to a thickness of about ¼ inch/4 mm. Cut out the required shapes, place them slightly apart on your lined baking sheets and bake for 12–15 minutes until golden. Leave to cool slightly on the baking sheets before transferring them to a wire rack to cool completely.

6   To decorate, divide the royal icing into as many colors as you want and tint with the gels. Place each colored royal icing in a separate decorating bag and decorate to your heart's content. I like to create 2 dots for eyes and place the silver dragées on top. Let them to dry before showing them to people and laughing loudly.

Lemon Cookies

I think lemon and almond go particularly well together. These are really easy to make and as an added extra, don't even need rolling out. They are also very versatile. Don't eat them while still warm: the lemon curd will still be molten hot!

½ cup superfine sugar
scant 2 sticks butter, softened
½ cup confectioners' sugar
1 large free-range egg yolk
1½ cups ground almonds
1 tsp almond extract
Finely grated zest and juice of 1 large unwaxed lemon
2 cups all-purpose flour
1 tsp baking powder
1 x small jar of lemon curd (you'll need about ⅓ cup)

1   Preheat the oven to 375°F and line two baking sheets with silicone liners.

2   Beat the superfine sugar and butter together in a large bowl until very pale and fluffy. Beat in the confectioners' sugar, egg yolk, ground almonds, almond extract, zest and 2 tsp of the lemon juice. Give it a good thrashing. Sift in the flour and baking powder and stir until everything is combined.

3   Form a blob of the mixture into a ball just a bit smaller than a golf ball and place on your lined baking sheets. Keep going, leaving a space between all your golf balls. With your thumb, squish down to form a little well in the now flattened ball and fill with a little dollop of lemon curd (not too much or it will overflow and burn).

4   Bake for about 10–12 minutes until the cookies are golden and gorgeous. Transfer to a wire rack to cool.

Made double batch on 5-16-16: used 1 jar + a little more of Lemon curd   (10 oz)

Yield: 53 +/- . Make them a little smaller next time. Could probably get 65-70 cookies.

Very yummy!

Ginger Cookies

Makes
1
batch

These are the unsophisticated, gorgeously moreish cookies that positively reek of ground ginger and which are very popular with both children and adults. A cookie with no drawbacks as far as I am concerned.

1 cup self-rising flour
½ tsp baking soda
2 tsp ground ginger
1 tsp ground cinnamon
2 tsp superfine sugar
½ stick butter
2 tbsp corn syrup

1 Preheat the oven to 375°F and line two baking sheets with silicone liners.

2 Sift together all the dry ingredients in a large bowl. Heat the butter and corn syrup gently in a pan and when the butter has melted, pour it over the dry ingredients. Mix well until you have a soft dough. If it's a little bit sticky, sprinkle a little more flour onto it until you get a consistency you can comfortably handle.

3 Using your hands, form small balls of the mixture, flatten them slightly and place them on your lined baking sheets, allowing a little space between them as they spread. Bake for about 15 minutes until golden and gorgeous-looking.

4 Let the cookies cool and harden on the baking sheets for a bit before lifting them onto wire racks to cool completely.

These cookies make great gifts: simply wrap in clean baking parchment and tie with a ribbon.

Chocolate Chip Shortbread

This is a really easy way of jazzing up plain shortbread. If you're feeling adventurous you could experiment with different flavored chocolate chips.

2¼ sticks butter, softened,
¼ cup superfine sugar
1¾ cups all-purpose flour
scant 1 cup cornstarch
¼ cup chunky chocolate chips

1 Cream the butter and sugar together in a large bowl until pale and fluffy. Sift the flour and cornstarch onto the butter mixture and mix until you have a lovely smooth dough.

2 Sprinkle the chocolate chips over the dough and knead in with your lovely clean hands until the chocolate is evenly distributed.

3 Roll out a sheet of plastic wrap, tip the dough onto it, then form the dough into a fat sausage and wrap up tightly. Leave to chill in the refrigerator for at least an hour.

4 Preheat the oven to 325°F and line two baking sheets with silicone liners.

5 Remove the roll of dough from its plastic wrap and slice into circles. Place the circles on your lined baking sheets and bake for about 30 minutes until they are pale golden. Leave the shortbread to cool on wire racks.

Rocky Roadsters

Although the rocky road combination of nuts, marshmallows and chocolate usually goes into ice cream, there's no reason why you shouldn't throw the trio into a muffin instead. If you do, you'll find yourself with an irresistible batch of the squishiest, meltiest, chunkiest muffins you've ever seen.

2 cups self-rising flour
1 tsp baking powder
3 tbsp cocoa powder
2¾ oz milk chocolate, chopped
½ cup walnut pieces
2 oz mini marshmallows (or large marshmallows snipped into pieces)
⅔ cup soft brown sugar
Generous ¾ cup milk
2 eggs, beaten
Scant ½ cup butter, melted

1   Preheat the oven to 400°F. Grease or line a 12-hole muffin pan.

2   Combine the flour, baking powder and cocoa and sift into a large bowl. Reserve about one-third of the chocolate chunks and nuts, then add the rest, along with the marshmallows, to the flour.

3   In a separate bowl or jug, combine the sugar, milk, eggs and butter, then pour into the dry ingredients. Stir together until just combined, then spoon big dollops of the batter into the prepared muffin pan. Gently press the reserved chocolate and nuts at random into the muffins.

4   Bake for about 20 minutes until risen and firm to the touch. Leave to cool in the pan for a few minutes, then transfer to a wire rack to cool.

Chirpy Chirpy Cheep Cheep

I love those little fluffy yellow chicks that appear in stores just before Easter. If you don't want to do anything other than ice some cupcakes, you could stand one of these chicks on top. Just make sure that no one thinks that they are edible. Otherwise these simple piped chicks look lovely. Pastel colors really do look better here.

Generous ¾ cup self-rising flour, sifted
½ cup superfine sugar, sifted
½ cup margarine, softened
1 tsp baking powder
2 large free-range eggs
1 tsp pure vanilla extract

For the decoration
1 quantity of glacé frosting (see page 32) tinted in pastel colors with gel food coloring
2 tbsp royal icing (see page 33) plus 1 tbsp green royal icing (optional)
yellow, black and orange gel food coloring
3 decorating bags with fine tubes

1 Preheat the oven to 325°F. Line a 12-hole muffin pan with baking cups. Put all the ingredients (except the decoration) in a mixer (food processor, food mixer, or just a big bowl with an electric whisk). Mix really well until the batter is light and fluffy. Put heaped teaspoons of the batter into the prepared cases, and bake in the oven for about 20 minutes until golden, and firm and springy when you give them a light prod on top. Let them cool before preparing the frosting—on a wire rack if you want, but not 100 percent necessary.

2 Make the cupcakes and leave them to cool. Ice the cooled cupcakes with a selection of pastel-colored frostings in glacé or fondant. Leave them to dry.

3 Split the royal icing into thirds. Take two-thirds and tint it yellow with gel food coloring. Fill a decorating bag with the yellow royal icing, and push to the end. To make a fluffy chick, pipe a chick shape onto the cake, and fill in the chick with random squiggles of

yellow royal icing. Make sure that you go ever so slightly over your outline, so that the chick looks really fluffy. To make a flatter chick, again pipe an outline. Thin out some of the yellow royal icing with a few drops of water so that you have a consistency a bit thicker than heavy cream. Carefully fill in the outline with this mixture, and leave to dry completely.

4 When both are dry, divide the remaining royal icing into two, and tint one portion black and the other orange. Fill two separate decorating bags, one with the black and one with the orange. Pipe an eye on each chick (two if the chick is not in profile!) with the black royal icing, and a beak with the orange.

5 If you have any extra royal icing, tint it another color (green looks good), and pipe tiny spots all the way round the outer edge of the cupcakes.

Party Time!

Kids' parties are often great fun for the little ones and a huge amount of stress for the parents! With these fantastic recipes and decorating ideas you'll be sure to have the delicious party treats covered—now all you need is some party games.

Lemony lusters
Makes 12

Edible luster comes as a powder in tiny tubes from sugarcraft stores. Be sure to check that it is edible and not just safe for removable cake decorations!

1 stick butter, softened
½ cup superfine sugar
2 large free-range eggs, beaten
Generous ¾ cup self-rising flour, sifted
1 tsp baking powder
Grated zest of 1 unwaxed lemon
1 tbsp freshly squeezed lemon juice

For the decoration
1 quantity glacé frosting (page 32)
Gel food coloring (optional)
1 tbsp royal icing (see page 33)
Edible luster (available from cake decorating and sugarcraft stores)
½ tsp vodka or other clear alcohol (this evaporates, don't worry!)
You will need a small paintbrush

1   Preheat the oven to 325°F. Line a 12-hole muffin pan with baking cups. Cream the butter and sugar together until really pale and fluffy. Slowly add the beaten eggs, beating well after each addition. Sift the flour and baking powder onto the mixture and, using a large metal spoon, carefully fold it in. Add the lemon zest and, if the batter looks a little stiff, add the juice a little at a time (it may not be necessary).

2   Fold again. The batter should gently plop off the spoon. Spoon into the prepared cases and bake for 20–25 minutes until golden and firm to the touch. Remove from the oven and leave to cool.

3   Make the glacé frosting (see page 32) and color as required. Spoon over the cooled cakes. When the frosting has dried, put the royal icing into a decorating bag with a fine tube, and pipe a large heart onto each cupcake. Wait for this to harden slightly, which will take around an hour.

4   To finish, tip ½ tsp of the luster onto a saucer or into a small bowl. Add some vodka to the luster drop by drop. Mix with the paintbrush until you have a consistency just a tiny bit looser than a paste. Leave the alcohol to evaporate—the mixture will thicken up slightly. Carefully brush the luster mixture over the piped heart and let it dry.

Decorating fun!
For a fun kids' party try baking plain cupcakes and providing the guests with frosting and sprinkles to create their very own masterpieces!

Boys' own
Makes 12

I like the idea of a masculine cupcake! Well, if there are cupcakes with frocks and shoes, it's only fair that the chaps should have something. Let us not forget that men are huge consumers of cake, although they may pretend they aren't that bothered.

1 quantity of base cupcakes (see page 166)
1 quantity glacé frosting (see page 32)
Gel food coloring in assorted colors
2 tbsp royal icing (see page 33)
3 decorating bags fitted with fine tubes

1 Make the cupcakes according to the recipe and leave to cool.

2 Make the glacé frosting (see page 32) with the confectioners' sugar and either lemon juice or water. Color the frosting a really deep blue or green or brown. Cover the cakes with the frosting and let them dry really well. With color this dark, it is important that the frosting is as dry as possible before you start decorating.

3 Divide the royal icing into three bowls, and tint them whatever color the chap likes. The royal icing needs to be really firm, so if it's a bit on the loose side add a little more sifted confectioners' sugar. Pipe on appropriately butch comic-strip type words, such as "BIFF", "POW" and "ZAP". Word of warning: if you pipe on the words before the frosting underneath has dried, or if the royal icing is too wet, the colors will bleed into each other.

Butterflies go disco
Makes 12

I have developed a growing stash of cutters. The glitter butterfly remains a firm favorite.

1 quantity of base cupcakes (see page 166)
1 quantity glacé frosting (see page 32)
Food coloring (preferably gel)
Cornstarch for dusting
Golf ball-sized piece of rolled fondant/ sugarpaste
Edible glue
Edible glitter
You will need butterfly cutters (large, small or both) and a paintbrush

1 Make the cupcakes according to whichever recipe you choose, and leave to cool. Make up the glacé frosting (see page 32) and color as you wish. Pour over the cakes and leave to dry.

2 Dust a little cornstarch onto a work surface, and roll out the rolled fondant until it is about 1/8 in thick. Cut out butterflies—allow one large butterfly per cake or two small.

3 Brush a little edible glue all over the butterflies and dip onto the edible glitter that you have poured onto a plate.

4 Stick the butterflies to the cakes. If you are using two small ones, it looks lovely if you have them flying off in different directions.

Peanut butter & choc chip cheekies
Makes 12

Kids just love these big fat muffins studded with chocolate chips and little nuggets of peanut. Throw a batch in the oven after school and they can enjoy them warm with a big glass of milk. If you want to go for a dairy-free version, use bittersweet chocolate chips and substitute soya milk for regular milk.

2 cups self-rising flour
1 tsp baking powder
3½ oz milk chocolate chips
Generous ⅔ cup crunchy peanut butter
⅔ cup soft brown sugar
2 eggs, beaten
Generous ¾ cup milk

1 Preheat the oven to 400°F. Grease or line a 12-hole muffin pan.

2 Combine the flour and baking powder and sift into a large bowl, then add about three-quarters of the chocolate chips.

3 In a separate bowl, beat together the peanut butter and sugar, then gradually beat in the eggs and milk to make a smooth mixture. Pour into the dry ingredients and stir together until just combined, then spoon large dollops into the prepared muffin pan. Sprinkle with the remaining chocolate chips, pressing them gently into the batter.

4 Bake for about 18 minutes until risen and golden. Leave to cool in the pan for a few minutes, then transfer to a wire rack to cool.

Beet bonanza
Makes 12

Don't be put off if you don't like beets, these perfectly pink muffins are not a million miles away from a carrot-cakey muffin—sweet, tender, moreish and, even better, bright pink! Serve them with a simple swirl of frosting or, for something a bit more special, look out for pink sugar sprinkles to scatter over the top.

2 cups all-purpose flour
1 tbsp baking powder
Scant ⅔ cup superfine sugar
1 tsp ground cinnamon
½ tsp ground ginger
Generous ¾ cup milk
2 large eggs, beaten
Scant ½ cup vegetable oil
Largish beet, grated (about 3½ oz)

For the frosting
5 oz cream cheese
4½ tbsp confectioners' sugar
1 tsp lemon juice
Pink food coloring

1 Preheat the oven to 400°F. Grease or line a 12-hole muffin pan.

2 Combine the flour, baking powder, superfine sugar, cinnamon and ginger and sift into a large bowl.

3 In a separate bowl, combine the milk, eggs and oil, then stir in the beet so that the mixture turns bright pink. Pour into the dry ingredients and stir together until just combined, then spoon large dollops of the batter into the prepared muffin pan.

4 Bake for about 20 minutes until risen and firm to the touch. Leave to cool in the pan for a few minutes, then transfer the muffins to a wire rack to cool.

5 To serve, beat together the cream cheese, confectioners' sugar and lemon juice until smooth and creamy. Add a few drops of pink food coloring to make a vibrant pink frosting, then swirl on top of the muffins.

Colored candies
Makes 12

These muffins are kiddie-tastic and will appeal to really little ones as much as older kids—particularly the way the candies turn the muffins rainbow-colored once they've been baked. Little-uns can help out with spooning on the frosting and sticking on M&Ms, while older kids can pretty much do it all themselves.

2 cups self-rising flour
1 tsp baking powder
½ cup superfine sugar
2 oz M&Ms
generous ¾ cup buttermilk
1 egg, beaten
1 tsp vanilla extract
Scant ½ cup butter, melted

To decorate

Scant ⅓ cup sour cream
1 cup confectioners' sugar, sifted
2 oz M&Ms

1 Preheat the oven to 375°F. Grease or line a 12-hole muffin pan.

2 Combine the flour, baking powder and superfine sugar and sift into a large bowl, then add the M&Ms.

3 In a separate bowl or jug, lightly beat the buttermilk, egg and vanilla to combine, then stir in the butter. Pour into the dry ingredients and stir together until just combined, then spoon big dollops of the batter into the prepared muffin pan.

4 Bake for about 20 minutes until risen and golden. Leave to cool in the pan for a few minutes, then transfer the muffins to a wire rack to cool completely.

5 To decorate, beat the sour cream and confectioners' sugar together until creamy, then spoon over the muffins. Decorate with more M&Ms on top.

Birthday mini muffins
Makes 24

Who needs a birthday cake when there are mini muffins to gobble instead? With twenty-four muffins in each batch, they're just perfect for a party—or for a very greedy birthday boy or girl!

2 cups self-rising flour
1 tsp baking powder
2 tbsp cocoa powder, plus extra for dusting
⅔ cup superfine sugar
3½ oz bittersweet chocolate, chopped
1 egg, beaten
Generous 1 cup plain yogurt
2 tbsp milk
Scant ½ cup butter, melted
24 birthday candles to decorate

1 Preheat the oven to 375°F. Grease or line a 24-hole mini muffin pan.

2 Combine the flour, baking powder, cocoa and superfine sugar and sift into a large bowl, then add the chocolate.

3 In a separate bowl or jug, combine the egg, yogurt, milk and butter, then pour into the dry ingredients. Stir together until just combined, then spoon large dollops of the batter into the prepared muffin pan, making sure there are plenty of chocolate chunks peeping through the tops of the muffins.

4 Bake for about 15 minutes until risen and firm to the touch. Leave to cool in the pan for a few minutes, then transfer to a wire rack to cool completely.

5 To serve, dust with cocoa and stick a candle in the center of each muffin. Light and enjoy!

Savory Treats & Breads

Four-seed Pesto Sensations

Makes
12

Scented with herby pesto and heaving with seeds, these yummy, wholesome-looking muffins are packed with healthy oils to keep you fighting fit and bouncing bright. Serve them as an accompaniment to a meal, or pop one in your lunchbox.

2 cups all-purpose flour
1 tbsp baking powder
1 tbsp superfine sugar
½ tsp salt
2 tbsp sesame seeds
2 tbsp sunflower seeds
2 tbsp pumpkin seeds
2 tbsp poppy seeds
2 eggs, beaten
4 tbsp olive oil
3 tbsp pesto
¾ cup milk
Ground black pepper

For the topping
2 tsp sesame seeds
2 tsp sunflower seeds
2 tsp pumpkin seeds
2 tsp poppy seeds

1 Preheat the oven to 400°F. Grease or line a 12-hole muffin pan.

2 Combine the seeds for the topping in a bowl and set aside.

3 Combine the flour, baking powder, sugar and salt and sift into a large bowl, then sprinkle the seeds over the top.

4 In a separate bowl or jug, lightly beat together the eggs, olive oil, pesto and milk and add a good grinding of black pepper. Pour into the dry ingredients and stir together until just combined.

5 Spoon large dollops of the batter into the prepared muffin pan, then sprinkle with the reserved topping seeds.

6 Bake for about 20 minutes until risen and golden. Leave to cool in the pan for a few minutes, then transfer the muffins to a wire rack to cool completely.

Sun-dried Tomato & Oregano Muffins

Makes 12

Serve these yummy muffins warm or cold topped with sprigs of fresh oregano, and lose yourself in those rich Mediterranean flavors. For extra indulgence, split open a warm muffin and spread with herby cream cheese.

2 cups all-purpose flour
1 tbsp baking powder
½ tsp salt
3 tbsp freshly grated Parmesan, plus extra for sprinkling
1 egg, beaten
Generous 1 cup milk
6 tbsp olive oil
6 sun-dried tomatoes, roughly chopped, plus 1 extra for sprinkling
1 garlic clove, finely chopped
1 tsp fresh oregano
Ground black pepper

1   Preheat the oven to 375°F. Grease or line a 12-hole muffin pan.

2   Combine the flour, baking powder and salt and sift into a large bowl, then sprinkle the Parmesan into the bowl.

3   In a separate bowl, lightly beat together the egg, milk and oil to combine, then stir in the tomatoes, garlic and oregano. Add a good grinding of black pepper, then pour into the dry ingredients and stir until just combined.

4   Spoon big dollops of the batter into the prepared muffin pan and sprinkle Parmesan and a few pieces of sun-dried tomato over each one, then grind over more black pepper.

5   Bake for about 20 minutes until well risen and golden. Leave to cool in the pan for a couple of minutes, then transfer the muffins to a wire rack to cool completely.

You could try other Mediterranean herbs such as basil or thyme too.

Roast Pepper & Black Olive Muffins

Makes 12

Add a splash of color to your muffin repertoire with these gorgeous cornmeal muffins. Chunks of sweet juicy pepper, shiny black olives and the bite of black pepper make these utterly moreish. They're fuss-free, too, if you use bottled roasted peppers—although if you want to roast your own, go right ahead.

Generous 1⅓ cups all-purpose flour
⅔ cup cornmeal
1 tbsp baking powder
1 tbsp superfine sugar
½ tsp salt
¾ cup buttermilk
2 eggs, beaten
Scant ½ cup butter, melted
4 large pieces of bottled roasted pepper, chopped (about 4½ oz)
½ cup pitted black olives, halved
Ground black pepper

1 Preheat the oven to 400°F. Grease or line a 12-hole muffin pan.

2 Combine the flour, cornmeal, baking powder, sugar and salt and sift into a large bowl.

3 In a separate bowl, combine the buttermilk, eggs and butter with about two-thirds of the roasted peppers and olives, and add a good grinding of black pepper. Pour into the dry ingredients and stir together until just combined

4 Spoon big dollops of the batter into the prepared muffin pan. Press the remaining roasted peppers and olives into the tops of the muffins and grind over more black pepper.

5 Bake for about 20 minutes until risen and golden. Leave to cool in the pan for a few minutes, then transfer to a wire rack to cool.

Smoked Salmon Muffins

In all honesty, muffins probably aren't the most sophisticated baked treat known to mankind. But these ones made with smoked salmon and cream cheese are doing their level best! Try serving them as a quirky savory for afternoon tea—something of a mix between smoked salmon sandwiches and freshly baked scones...

2 cups all-purpose flour
1 tbsp baking powder
1 tbsp superfine sugar
½ tsp salt
2¾ oz cream cheese, plus extra to serve
Generous ¾ cup milk
1 large egg, beaten
¼ cup butter, melted
3½ oz smoked salmon, snipped into small pieces
2 scallions, chopped
1 tsp fresh dill, chopped
Ground black pepper
Fresh dill sprigs to garnish

1 Preheat the oven to 400°F. Grease or line a 12-hole muffin pan.

2 Mix the flour, baking powder, sugar and salt together and sift into a large bowl.

3 In a separate bowl, beat the cream cheese until soft, then gradually beat in the milk until smooth and creamy. Stir in the egg and butter, followed by the salmon, scallions, dill and a good grinding of black pepper. Pour into the dry ingredients and stir until just combined, then spoon big dollops of the batter into the prepared muffin pan and grind over a little more black pepper.

4 Bake for about 20 minutes until risen and golden. Leave to cool in the pan for a few minutes, then transfer to a wire rack to cool.

5 Serve spread with more cream cheese and dill sprigs to decorate.

Zucchini, Feta & Scallion Cupcakes

Makes about 12

The great hunks of feta in these cupcakes are a lovely surprise. The zucchini adds moisture and flavor, as well as beautiful flecks of green. These go well with a really piquant salsa. The batter is very stiff, almost dough-like. Don't worry and don't add more milk. The zucchini sorts out the texture. Have faith.

scant 1½ cups all-purpose flour
2 tbsp sugar
3 tsp baking powder
½ tsp salt
1 small zucchini, grated
2 scallions, finely chopped
1 cup ricotta cheese
5 oz feta cheese, crumbled into chunks
2 large free-range eggs, lightly beaten
½ cup butter, melted
¼ cup milk

1 Preheat the oven to 400°F. Line a 12-hole muffin pan with cupcake liners.

2 Sift the flour, sugar, baking powder and salt into a large bowl, and mix through well. In another bowl, mix the zucchini, scallions, ricotta, feta, eggs, melted butter and the milk. Give it a bit of a beat around, then add to the dry ingredients. The batter will be stiff.

3 Spoon the batter into the prepared cases, take the worried look off your face and put them in the oven. Bake in the oven for 20–25 minutes or until firm to the touch and golden brown. Eat warm..

Perfect for picnics, lunchboxes or a summer lunch with friends.

Cheddar & Rosemary Bread

This lovely loaf can be made freeform to have hunks torn off for lunch, or baked in a loaf pan for thin slices, buttered and quartered and presented nicely on a plate for afternoon tea. The herb doesn't have to be rosemary—thyme would also be great—and the cheese doesn't have to be Cheddar. Any hard cheese with plenty of flavor would be fine.

3½ cups white bread flour
1 tsp salt
1 tsp superfine sugar
3 tsp English mustard powder
⅓ oz dried yeast
1¼ cups tepid water
2 tsp fresh rosemary, chopped
10 ½ cups grated strong Cheddar cheese

1 In a large bowl, stir together the flour, salt, sugar, mustard powder and yeast, then add the water and mix until a dough forms. Tip the dough onto a well-floured work surface and get kneading like you mean it for at least 10 minutes, but maybe 15. You may stop when the dough is smooth and elastic and doesn't feel straggly under your fingers. Form the dough into a ball and score a large, deep cross in the top. Put it back in the bowl, cover with a tea towel and leave somewhere warm to rise—this will probably take about 1 hour.

2 When the dough has doubled in size, bash it about to knock out all the air and start kneading again, this time adding 1⅔ cups of the grated cheese in three goes. Just sprinkle a third over the dough and start kneading; when it has been incorporated, add the next third and

so on. When all the cheese is in, knead the dough for another 5 minutes before either forming it into a loose shape and placing on a baking sheet, or putting it into a greased and floured 2¼ lb/1 kg pan. Make lots of dimpled holes in the top of the loaf with your fingers, sprinkle the mustard powder and remaining cheese over the top and prod in a bit more. Cover the dough again with the tea towel and leave once more in the warm place to rise for another hour.

3 Preheat the oven to 375°F. The baking time depends on what shape you have made, but it should be around the 20-minute mark. You will know when it is done by tapping the bottom of the loaf. If it sounds hollow, it is ready. If you have cooked it in a pan, turn out onto a wire rack to cool.

Beautiful Bread

There is nothing quite like the taste of a handmade, homemade loaf of bread fresh out of the oven. Breakfast, brunch, lunch or dinner, fresh bread is always a welcome addition to the table!

Basic white bread
Makes 1 loaf

This is easy to make, does not require a bread machine, and gives the home baker a base from which to experiment.

3⅔ cups white bread flour
A large pinch of sea salt
½ oz instant/active dry or fresh yeast
Scant 1 cup warm water
1 medium egg
Scant ½ cup milk

1 Place the flour in a large bowl, add the salt and mix well. If using instant yeast, pour it over the flour (if using fresh yeast, whisk it into the warm water; make sure the water is the temperature of a tepid bath, if it is any hotter you will kill the yeast).

2 Make a well in the middle of the flour and, using a wooden spoon, add the warm (see above) water (or warm water and fresh yeast), mixing until you have a slightly soggy-looking paste. Tip this paste onto a well-floured surface, then knead for 10–15 minutes, adding flour if necessary, until the dough becomes firm and elastic and ceases to stick to the work surface.

3 Put the dough into a floured mixing bowl, cover with a clean damp cloth and put it in a warm place such as an airing cupboard for 1 hour.

4 Remove the dough from the mixing bowl and place it on a floured work surface. Form it into a sausage shape and put it into a non-stick baking pan. The dough should come two-thirds of the way up the inside of the pan.

5 Beat the egg and milk together, then paint the top of the dough with this eggwash. Allow to rise for 30–40 minutes until the dough comes above the top of the baking pan.

6 Preheat the oven to 425°F. Brush the top of the dough again lightly with the eggwash and bake on a baking sheet for 10 minutes, then turn the oven down to 350°F and bake for a further 20 minutes.

7 Tip the bread out and check that the sides and bottom of the loaf are fully baked. Leave to cool on a wire rack for 1 hour before cutting.

Brewery bread with crystal malt
Makes 1 loaf

By making bread using beer as both the liquid and the raising agent, you are creating something with a unique flavor. One of the most important ingredients in the production of British real ale is malted barley. Different strengths of malted barley produce different flavored and different colored beers, and my favorite is golden crystal malt. I love to sprinkle this delicious, crunchy malt over this bread just before it goes into the oven. The results are fantastic.

1½ cups
whole-wheat bread flour
1⅔ cups white bread flour
1 handful crystal malt
1 tbsp salt
¾ oz instant/active dry yeast
2½ tbsp butter, melted
1¼ cups good local beer
1 egg for eggwash
Onion seeds
Sea salt

1 Mix all the dry ingredients except the onion seeds and salt together in a large bowl, then make a well in the center and pour in the melted butter and beer. Stir to form a dough.

2 Tip the dough out onto a lightly floured work surface and knead for 10 minutes, then put it back into the bowl and leave it to rest in a warm place for 1 hour.

3 Return the dough to the floured work surface and shape it into a ball, then flatten it and roll it up. Put the dough on a greased baking sheet and leave it to rise for a further hour.

4 Preheat the oven to 400°F. Beat the egg. Cut several slashes across the top of the bread and glaze with the egg. Sprinkle liberally with onion seeds and sea salt. Bake for 30 minutes, then transfer to a wire rack to cool.

Buttermilk oaten bread
Makes 2 small loaves

Fine oatmeal gives a wonderful gritty texture to this favorite Irish bread. Buttermilk was once a staple ingredient in breads and cakes, and gave a slightly sour taste and good keeping qualities. Serve this as a satisfying part of "high tea", warm with cheese or toasted with melting butter and thick fruity jams.

Generous 1 cup fine oatmeal
1¼ cups buttermilk
½ cup milk
1¾ cups all-purpose flour, sifted
1 tsp baking powder
¼ tsp salt

1 Soak the oatmeal in the buttermilk and milk overnight. The following day preheat the oven to 350°F.

2 Grease a baking sheet. Mix together the flour, baking powder and salt. Add the oatmeal and milk mixture and mix well to give a soft dough. Knead until smooth.

3 Divide into two portions and, on a floured board, roll each portion out to a thickness of about 1 in and about 4 in in diameter. Place both loaves on the prepared sheet and bake for 35–40 minutes until they are golden and sound hollow when tapped. Remove from the oven and serve hot with butter.

Sesame rolls

Makes 14

From Trerice in Cornwall, these little rolls enjoy the sweet nuttiness of sesame and are delicious at teatime filled with smoked salmon or honey roast ham. The glory of Trerice is the south-facing drawing room—a perfect room in which to take tea. Displayed here are some fine examples of Chinese porcelain tea bowls and little pots that were imported on the same ships that brought the chests of tea from the Orient. European potters were amazed at the fine, translucent quality of the Chinese wares when they first came across them in the middle of the 17th century and spent the following fifty years or so attempting to manufacture something equally beautiful.

½ oz fresh yeast (to substitute dried yeast, see page 36)
2 tsp superfine sugar
1¾ cups water, warmed
4¾ cups white bread flour, sifted
1½ tsp full-cream milk powder (Coffeemate or similar)
½ tsp salt
¼ stick butter, softened
1 egg, beaten and mixed with a little water
2–3 tbsp sesame seeds

1 Mix together the yeast, sugar and 6 tbsp of the water. Leave in a warm place for about 20–30 minutes until frothy.

2 Mix together the flour, milk powder and salt and rub in the fat. Add the yeast mixture and the remaining water and mix to a pliable dough. Knead until smooth and elastic, then place in a bowl, cover with a damp cloth and leave in a warm place for 1–1½ hours until doubled in size.

3 Grease two baking sheets. When the dough is well risen, divide into 2½ oz pieces, form these into bun shapes and place on the prepared sheets. Brush the tops with eggwash and sprinkle liberally with sesame seeds. Leave in a warm place for about 30 minutes until well risen.

4 Preheat the oven to 400°F. When the rolls are well risen, bake for 20–25 minutes until golden brown and firm. Remove from the oven and lift onto a wire rack to cool. Serve warm or cold. If liked stir 1 tbsp of sesame seeds into the dough with the yeast mixture. Sprinkle as above with more seeds before baking.

Historically, white bread was purely for the wealthy and was a status symbol, which today we take for granted. The bread that the peasants ate would have been coarse whole-wheat, containing large amounts of husk and impurities.

Boxty bread
Makes 2 small round flat loaves

Boxty bread is traditional festive Irish bread, flat and round and marked into four portions before baking to allow for easy division once cooked. With potatoes its essentially Irish ingredient, it was once an indulgence for Shrove Tuesday, All Saints' Day or Halloween.

8 oz raw potatoes
8 oz mashed potatoes
1⅔ cups all-purpose flour, sifted
¼ cup butter, melted
Salt and freshly ground black pepper

1 Preheat the oven to 375°F. Grease a baking sheet. Wash and peel the raw potatoes. Grate into a clean cloth and wring well over a bowl to squeeze out the juice. Place the grated potatoes in a bowl with the mashed potatoes and mix together. Leave the starchy liquid in the bowl until the starch has settled, then pour off the liquid and add the starch to the potatoes. Add the flour, melted butter and seasoning and mix to a soft dough. Knead well.

2 Divide into two portions and, on a floured board, roll into flat circles. Place on the baking sheet and divide the top of each loaf into four with a sharp knife. Bake for 40 minutes until firm and golden. Remove from the oven and serve hot with butter.

Irish soda bread
Makes 1 loaf

Soda bread is unique. Traditionally a poor-man's bread from Ireland, it has now attained something akin to cult status. Nothing quite compares to the nutty aroma of baking or cooling soda bread. It has great advantages for the modern cook over normal types of bread, in that it requires no rising. The basic principle, of course, is that it uses baking soda and buttermilk in place of yeast. The most important thing to remember when making it is to do as little kneading as possible; the looser the dough, the better. Traditionally, the cross-shaped cut on top of the soda bread was made to bless the bread and the corners were pricked to allow the fairies to escape.

3¼ cups white bread flour (to make brown soda bread, use half whole-wheat flour and half white bread flour)
1 tsp salt
1 tsp baking soda
1½–1¾ cups sour milk or buttermilk, to mix

1 Preheat the oven to 450°F. Sift the dry ingredients into a bowl. Make a well in the center. Pour most of the milk in, then using one hand, mix in the flour from the sides of the bowl, adding more milk if necessary. The dough should be softish, not too wet and sticky.

2 When it all comes together, turn it out on to a well-floured work surface, then pat the dough into a circle about 1½ in thick. Put a cross on it and prick the corners. Put on a baking sheet.

3 Bake for 15 minutes, then turn the oven down to 400°F and bake for a further 30 minutes or until cooked. If you are in doubt, tap the bottom of the bread—if it is cooked, it will sound hollow. Cool on a wire rack.

Organic whole-wheat bread
Makes 2 x 2 lb loaves

This lovely nutty-flavored bread comes from Branscombe Bakery, the last traditional bakery to be used in Devon. Until 1987 it was run by brothers Gerald and Stuart Collier who baked bread, buns, cakes, tarts and scones every day of the year. The oven was lit at four o'clock every morning and then, three hours later when it had reached the required temperature, the ashes were raked out, the oven cleaned and then the first batch of 130 loaves arranged inside.

1 oz fresh yeast (to substitute dried yeast, see page 36)
½ tsp light or dark soft brown sugar
2½–3 cups warm water (it should be almost hand-hot, and the amount needed varies according to the flour used)
6½ cups organic whole-wheat flour, sifted and warmed slightly in the oven
1 tbsp sea salt
1 tbsp corn or sunflower oil
1 tbsp clear honey

1 Cream together the yeast and sugar and blend with 4–6 tbsp of the warm water. Leave in a warm, draught-free place for 10–20 minutes until frothy.

2 Mix together the flour and salt and make a well in the middle. Pour in the oil, honey, yeast mixture and enough of the remaining water to give a soft, elastic dough. Knead with the hands for about 10 minutes. Shape the dough into a ball and place in a lightly greased bowl. Dust the top with a little flour, cover with a clean damp cloth and leave in a warm, draught-free place until almost doubled in size (50 minutes to 2 hours).

3 Grease two 2 lb loaf pans. Turn the dough out onto a lightly floured board and knead vigorously for 8–10 minutes. Divide the dough into two equal portions and shape to fit the pans. Place in the pans, sprinkle the tops with a little more flour and cover with a clean damp cloth. Leave in a warm place for a further 30–40 minutes until the dough reaches the top of the pans.

4 Preheat the oven to 425°F. When the dough has risen, bake the loaves for 30 minutes. Remove from the oven and remove from the pans. Place the loaves in the oven for a further 10–15 minutes until they sound hollow when tapped. Remove from the oven and cool on a wire rack.

Don't be tempted to cut into a fresh-baked loaf if it has only just come out of the oven. Not only are you likely to burn your fingers, it will be difficult to cut. Wait until the loaf has cooled to a comfortable "warm" temperature, which usually takes about half an hour.

A Lighter Bite

Gooseberry Fool Cake

This gooseberry-laden sponge marries brilliantly with the light-as-a-feather elderflower topping. Its high fruit content means that it's a good source of vitamins A and C. This cake is best made with the really tart, early season green gooseberries. You can use red or yellow varieties, but they are quite a lot sweeter. If fresh gooseberries are hard to find, you can use frozen ones. As it is so moist, this cake needs to be kept in the refrigerator. The frosting will wilt after a day or two— simply re-fluff it with a fork.

⅔ cup butter, melted, plus extra for brushing
Tapioca flour for dusting
5 eggs
1 cup light brown sugar
2 cups ground almonds
Scant 1 cup sorghum flour
1½ tsp gluten-free baking powder
1½ tsp guar gum
1 tsp vanilla extract
A pinch of salt
1 lb green gooseberries, topped, tailed, rinsed and dried

For the frosted berries
7 whole gooseberries, topped, tailed, rinsed and dried
1 tbsp pasteurized liquid egg white
1–2 tbsp superfine sugar

For the elderflower cream
scant 1 cup heavy cream
2 tbsp elderflower cordial
⅓ cup confectioners' sugar, sifted

1   Preheat the oven to 350°F. Line a 9 in round springform pan with a disc of parchment paper, then brush with melted butter and dust with tapioca flour.

2   Crack the eggs into a large mixing bowl and beat with an electric mixer on high speed. Add the melted butter and beat again. Add the sugar, almonds, sorghum flour, baking powder, guar gum, vanilla and salt, then beat until creamy. Stir in the gooseberries using a rubber spatula. Be gentle: you want to keep them intact.

3   Spoon the batter into the prepared pan and bang the pan firmly on a work surface to get rid of air pockets. Bake for 45 minutes until firm and springy to the touch. A flat cake skewer will come out clean when the cake is ready.

4   Leave the cake in its pan for 10–15 minutes, then turn it out, right way up, onto a rack covered with parchment paper. Leave to cool, then peel off the parchment. For the frosted berries, wash the gooseberries and pat them dry. Brush them lightly with egg white, then roll them in superfine sugar. Place the coated berries on a piece of parchment paper and leave to dry.

5   For the elderflower cream topping, whip the cream with the cordial and confectioners' sugar until it forms stiff peaks. Spread the cream over the cake with a palette knife: we like a rough peaked finish, but you could go super-sleek. Decorate with the frosted berries.

Raspberry Cake

This is simple to make, perfect for a summer's day. Once the topping is on, the cake should be quickly admired and then eaten before the cream slides off.

Melted butter for brushing
Tapioca flour for dusting
4 eggs
¾ cup light brown sugar
4½ oz hazelnuts, ground
1¾ oz cornmeal
¼ cup sorghum flour
1½ tsp gluten-free baking powder
1½ tsp guar gum and ¼ tsp salt
Generous 1 cup hazelnuts, toasted and chopped
5½ oz white chocolate, chopped
5–6 tbsp raspberry jam for filling
24 raspberries to decorate

For the roasted raspberries
7 oz raspberries
4 tbsp clear honey
½ tsp cinnamon sugar

For the cream filling & toppin
1 cup mascarpone
⅓ cup heavy cream
½ cup crème fraîche
½ cup confectioners' sugar
2 tsp lemon juice and 1 tsp vanilla extract

For the raspberry sugar
1 freeze-dried raspberry
1 tsp confectioners' sugar

1 Preheat the oven to 350°F. Brush 2 x 8 in round layer cake pans with melted butter and dust with tapioca flour.

2 For the roasted raspberries, put the berries in a baking pan, drizzle the honey over them and dredge with cinnamon sugar. Roast in the oven for 20 minutes. Leave to cool for 5 minutes.

3 Crack the eggs into a large bowl, then add the sugar, ground nuts, cornmeal, sorghum flour, baking powder, guar gum and salt. Beat with an electric mixer until creamy and stiff. Using a spatula, stir in the chopped nuts, white chocolate and roasted raspberries.

4 Divide the batter between the pans. Bake for 20–25 minutes, until a flat cake skewer comes out clean. Leave the cakes in the pans for a couple of minutes, then turn out onto a rack. Invert one so its flat bottom side is upwards.

5 For the cream filling, put the mascarpone, cream, crème fraîche, confectioners' sugar, lemon juice and vanilla into a bowl and beat with an electric mixer until stiff.

6 For the raspberry sugar, use the back of a spoon to crush the freeze-dried raspberry to a fine powder. Sift in the 1 tsp confectioners' sugar—if it is not pink enough, add a little more raspberry. Only mix little by little as you need it, as the freeze-dried raspberry goes soft after a couple of hours.

7 Spread 1 cake thickly with raspberry jam. Spread half the cream filling on top of the jam and place the second cake on top. Spread the remaining cream filling on top of the cake. Arrange the raspberries on top and dust the cake with raspberry sugar.

Upside-down Polenta Plum Cake

This is a great cake for using up any bumper seasonal fruit harvests. Instead of plums you could use damsons or peaches—or any fruit with a bit of body. The great thing about red-skinned plums (we use Victoria plums) is that you benefit from the gorgeous color contrast against the sunshine yellow of the cornmeal. The cake itself is not very sweet, but when it is turned upside down those lovely syrupy fruit juices seep into the sponge. Delicious served warm with homemade custard.

Scant ½ cup butter, melted, plus extra for brushing
2 eggs
1½ cups cornmeal
⅔ cup ground almonds
1½ tsp gluten-free baking powder
¾ tsp guar gum
¾ tsp vanilla extract
6½ oz rice syrup
Scant 1 cup crème fraîche
2 tbsp orange juice

For the topping
8 red plums, halved and pitted
4 tbsp light brown sugar
⅓ cup orange juice

1   Preheat the oven to 350°F. Brush a 2 lb loaf pan with melted butter, line with a silicone loaf pan liner, then liberally butter the loaf liner.

2   First, make the topping. Put the plums, skin side up, in a baking pan. Mix the brown sugar and orange juice and pour over the plums. Roast in the oven for about 15–17 minutes, until soft but still keeping their shape. Cool in the pan.

3   Crack the eggs into a large bowl, then add the cornmeal, almonds, baking powder, guar gum and vanilla extract. In another bowl, mix the melted butter with the rice syrup, crème fraîche and orange juice. Beat with an electric mixer at low speed until just combined. Don't worry if it looks a bit curdled. Pour this mixture over the dry ingredients and beat at high speed until smooth and pale.

4   Take the plums out of the pan and put them in the loaf pan, skin side down. Pour the syrup that remains in the baking pan into a measuring cup or jug and pour 4 tsp of the syrup over the plums in the loaf pan. Set the rest aside.

5   Spoon the cake batter into the loaf pan and spread it gently. Bake for 30 minutes, then cover with a disc of parchment paper and bake for a further 15–20 minutes until springy to the touch; a flat cake skewer will come out clean when the cake is ready. As soon as the cake comes out of the oven, loosen the sides with a knife, then place a serving plate upside down on top of the pan and turn over quickly. Remove from the pan and peel off the parchment paper. Spoon the remaining syrup from cooking the plums over the cake while it is still warm.

Custard Creams

Classic British custard creams have been reinterpreted in fabulous gluten-free form.

1½ sticks butter, softened and cubed
¾ cup superfine sugar
1¼ cups cornmeal
Generous 1½ cups ground almonds
Scant ¾ cup custard powder
1 egg
½ tsp vanilla extract
Tapioca flour for dusting

For the filling
1¼ sticks butter, softened
¾ cup confectioners' sugar
2 tbsp custard powder
½ tsp vanilla extract

To decorate
1–2 tbsp confectioners' sugar, sifted
You will need a decorating bag fitted with a small star tube

1   Preheat the oven to 325°F. Cut pieces of baking parchment to line the base of two large baking sheets.

2   Put the butter, sugar, cornmeal, almonds, custard powder, egg and vanilla into a large mixing bowl and beat using an electric mixer at low speed until the mixture forms a soft dough.

3   Dust your hands, rolling pin and work surface lightly with tapioca flour. Knead the dough gently and then roll out to about ¼ in thick. Using a pastry cutter (we used a 2½ in heart-shaped cutter), cut out the dough and place the shapes on the baking sheets. The cookies will spread as they bake, so make sure you leave plenty of space between them.

4   Bake for 12–14 minutes, until golden and firm to the touch (they get firmer as they cool). Leave on the baking sheets for 5–10 minutes, then transfer to a wire rack.

5   To make the filling, put the butter into a bowl. Sift the confectioners' sugar and custard powder into the bowl, add the vanilla and beat using an electric mixer at medium speed until smooth. Chill in the refrigerator for 30 minutes.

6   Spoon the filling into a decorating bag fitted with a small star tube. Turn half of the cookies upside down and pipe the cream in swirls on top. Cover with the remaining cookies—with the nice side facing upwards.

7   To decorate, place a paper doily over the cookies and dust with confectioners' sugar.

Cranberry, Pecan & Maple Syrup Flapjacks

Makes
15 pieces

These are generously laden with pecans, and the maple syrup marries really well with both the pecans and the cranberries. It really is worth going to the effort of toasting the pecans.

Generous 1½ sticks butter, plus extra, melted, for brushing
Generous ½ cup light brown sugar
3½ tbsp corn syrup
3 tbsp maple syrup
½ tsp salt
Generous 1¾ cups gluten-free oats
3½ oz gluten-free oat flour
1 cup pecan halves, toasted
½ cup pecan halves, toasted and chopped
3 oz millet flakes
Generous ½ cup dried cranberries
Finely grated zest of 1 orange
½ tsp orange oil

For the topping
3 tbsp dried cranberries
Finely grated zest of 1 orange
3 tbsp maple syrup

1   Preheat the oven to 325°F. Cut a rectangle of parchment paper to line the base of a 12 x 9 x 1½ in baking pan. Pop the parchment in the pan and brush it and the pan liberally with melted butter.

2   Put the butter, sugar, corn syrup, maple syrup and salt into a pan and melt over a low heat, stirring every minute or so with a wooden spoon. Cook for 8–10 minutes until all the sugar has dissolved (when the bottom of the pan no longer feels gritty, the mixture is ready). Don't let the mixture boil or the flapjacks will be hard.

3   Put the oats, oat flour, halved and chopped pecans, millet flakes, dried cranberries, orange zest and orange oil into a large bowl and stir. Pour in the melted butter mixture and stir well, using a rubber spatula. Ensure that all the dry ingredients are well coated.

4   Spoon the mixture into the pan and spread evenly, using a rubber spatula—you need to push it into the corners, but leave the surface fairly lumpy for a rustic effect. For the topping, scatter the cranberries over the surface, pressing them in lightly.

5   Bake for 15–17 minutes until golden with slightly darker edges. It will be bubbling and quite soft when you take it from the oven, but will firm up as it cools. Leave in the pan to cool for 10 minutes, then transfer to a wire rack.

6   Mix the grated orange zest with the maple syrup and drizzle it over the flapjack while it is still warm. Cut up into 15 slices.

Saintly Treats

Sometimes you need to rein in those calories, and let's face it, most cakes aren't too easy on the waistline. Here are some examples of really healthy, satisfying snacks that will give you a nutrient boost but still feel like a treat—and won't break the calorie bank if you're watching your weight.

Bananas-a-go-go cookies
Makes 1 batch

Right, these little chaps are pretty cool. Really easy to make, they are sugar and wheat free, the fat is "healthy" fat, and they are really banana-y! They are soft cookies, so if you are waiting for them to crisp up, you may be waiting a while, and they are also best eaten on the day you make them.

3 ripe bananas
6½ oz pitted dates, chopped
1 cup rolled jumbo oats
⅓ cup sunflower oil
1 tsp vanilla extract

1 Preheat the oven to 350°F and line two baking sheets with silicone liners.

2 Mash the bananas in a large bowl, then add the dates, oats, sunflower oil and vanilla, and give it a good mix. Leave the mixture to stand for 15–20 minutes to firm up a little and for the oats to absorb some of the liquid.

3 Drop teaspoons of the mixture onto your lined baking sheets and flatten with the back of a spoon—they don't spread much, so the shape you make on the sheet will be the shape of the finished cookie. Bake for 15–20 minutes then transfer the cookies to a wire rack to cool.

No-bake healthy humdingers
Makes 1 batch

This has got to be the ultimate in virtuous cookies. Yet again, I am pushing the boundaries about what actually constitutes a cookie. These aren't even cooked, for goodness' sake. There is not one ingredient here that a full-on wholefood addict would have a problem with, and they are actually great as sports snacks too, as they fill a gap and have lots of lovely slow-release sugar properties. Perfect.

½ cup sunflower seeds
1 tbsp tahini (sesame seed paste)
⅓ cup dry unsweetened/desiccated or shredded coconut
1 tbsp runny honey
1½ oz wheatgerm
2 oz dates, pitted and chopped

1 Bash the sunflower seeds a little in a mortar with a pestle or in a food processor. You just want to break them up a bit. Tip them into a large bowl and add all the other ingredients.

2 Form the mixture (easier to do this in 2 portions) into a roll, wrap tightly in plastic wrap and leave to chill in the refrigerator for a couple of hours. When you are ready, just slice pieces off.

Maple cloud cookies
Makes 1 batch

These cookies have a light and fluffy texture—something between a soft cookie and a muffin. I have included them because they are sugar free, and are suitable for those who are sugar-intolerant and diabetics, who often get ignored in the homemade cookie department. Sugar substitutes can be found in all supermarkets nowadays. It's usually in the sugar aisle.

1 stick butter, softened (although if push comes to shove you could use something like a soy margarine)
½ cup sour cream
4½ oz apple, peeled and grated
2 large free-range eggs
1 tsp maple syrup
½ tsp vanilla extract
1¾ cups all-purpose flour
⅓ cup sugar substitute
1 tsp baking soda
1 tsp baking powder

1 Preheat the oven to 375°F and line two baking sheets with silicone liners.

2 Mix the butter, sour cream, apple, eggs, maple syrup and vanilla together in a large bowl. In another bowl, sift in the flour, sugar substitute, baking soda and baking powder, then add the dry ingredients to the wet ingredients and mix very well. Drop dessertspoons of the mixture onto your lined baking sheets and bake for about 10 minutes until pale golden. Transfer the cookies to wire racks to cool.

Soft berry cookies
Makes 1 batch

These are just the most delicious, fruit-packed, oaty, soft cookies. They are easy to make and you can alter the fruit to whatever you can get your hands on. Wholefood stores and now most supermarkets sell a vast array of dried tropical fruit. I've made them with dried mangoes, raisins, figs, blueberries, pears—all work beautifully.

Generous ¼ cup sunflower oil
6 tbsp butter, softened
½ cup soft light brown sugar
1 large free-range egg
½ tsp vanilla extract
¾ cup jumbo oats
Scant 1 cup plain whole-wheat flour
½ tsp baking soda
½ tsp baking powder
½ tsp ground cinnamon
4 oz dried apple
1 oz cranberries
1 oz blueberries

1   Preheat the oven to 350°F and line two baking sheets with silicone liners.

2   Mix the sunflower oil, butter and sugar together in a large bowl. Beat in the egg and vanilla, then stir in the oats. Sift the flour, baking soda, baking powder and cinnamon over the sugar and oil mixture and mix in. Add the dried fruit and stir until they are just combined.

3   Drop dessertspoonfuls of the mixture onto your lined baking sheets, leaving lots of space between them as they spread and bake for about 10 minutes until pale golden. Leave on the baking sheets to harden and set a bit before cooling on wire racks.

Chewy date cookies
Makes 1 batch

Dates are just fantastic in cooking, and their intense sweetness means that you can reduce the amount of sugar you add to the recipe. These date lovelies still contain sugar, as it's important for the chewy factor. You can reduce the amount of sugar you use, but it will change the overall consistency. You could also use entirely whole-wheat flour instead of a mixture of white and brown. It is up to you.

¾ stick butter, softened
¾ cup soft light brown sugar
Finely grated zest of 1 large unwaxed lemon
1 large free-range egg
Generous ¾ cup all-purpose flour
½ cup whole-wheat flour
1 tsp baking powder
½ tsp grated nutmeg
1 tsp ground cinnamon
A pinch of salt
¼ cup milk
6½ oz pitted dates, chopped

1   Preheat the oven to 325°F and line two baking sheets with silicone liners.

2   Cream the butter and sugar together in a large bowl until light and fluffy, then add the zest and egg and beat away. In another bowl, sift together the flours, baking powder, nutmeg, cinnamon and salt. Add to the creamed mixture in alternate dollops with a little bit of milk and beat well between each addition. Finally stir in the dates.

3   Drop round dessertspoons of the mixture onto your lined baking sheets, leaving space between them as they spread, and bake for 12–15 minutes until golden brown. Transfer the cookies to wire racks to cool.

Peter Rabbit cookies
Makes 1 batch

Well, carrot cookies really. Fruit and vegetables in one cookie? Can this be true? Yes, I tell you, yes. Not at all "worthy"-tasting: carrot and ginger, crystallized papaya, cinnamon and a little hint of coconut, all make these truly delicious little morsels. I'm just going to have another one actually...

7 oz raw carrots, peeled and chopped
4 oz hard white vegetable fat
1 stick butter, softened
¾ cup soft light brown sugar
1 large free-range egg
2 cups all-purpose flour
1 tsp baking powder
1 tsp ground cinnamon
1 tsp ground ginger
½ cup dry unsweetened/desiccated or shredded coconut
2 oz candied/crystallized papaya

1 Cook the carrots in a pan of unsalted boiling water until tender and then purée in a blender. You need to avoid any lumps at all, so push it through a sieve if you are unsure whether your purée is smooth enough. Leave to cool until cold.

2 Preheat the oven to 400°F and line two baking sheets with silicone liners.

3 Beat the white fat, butter and sugar together in a large bowl. You may need to scrape the white fat off the bowl every now and again, as it does like to stick to the sides. When the mixture is looking pale and fluffy, add the egg and continue beating until everything is well amalgamated. Add the cold puréed carrots and mix in.

4 Sift the flour, baking powder, cinnamon and ginger onto the mixture and mix until incorporated. Finally mix in the coconut and papaya. Drop heaped teaspoons onto your lined baking sheets, then flatten and squidge them into thinnish circles with the back of a spoon. Bake for about 10 minutes until golden, then transfer to a wire rack to cool. Delicious.

Perfect in lunchboxes or to take to the office for a mid-morning nibble, these healthy cookies are also great for kids—they get fruit and vegetables all disguised as an indulgent treat.

Mildon flapjacks
Makes 1 batch

Flapjacks are just pushing the boundary of what is or what isn't a cookie, but my reckoning is that you would eat them as you would a cookie, so here they are. Thanks to my friend Helen who gave me her recipe. It's one where you get what, to my mind, is a proper flapjack—still slightly chewy and moist. Very comforting and the oats are amazingly good for you. We'll skip over the other ingredients' health benefits. But they must be good for your mental health. Surely …

Generous 1¼ sticks butter
1¼ cups superfine sugar
½ cup corn syrup
3¼ cups jumbo oats

1   Preheat the oven to 350°F and grease an 8 in square baking pan (if it's a bit bigger or rectangular, please don't worry, just go for it).

2   Melt the butter, sugar and corn syrup in a large pan. When melted, add the oats and stir in, then tip the whole lot into the pan and press down firmly. Bake for about 25 minutes until pale golden. It may look slightly undercooked and very soft, but it sets as it cools. The key is not to overcook the flapjack, as this way it remains chewy. If you cook it too much, it will be harder. When the flapjack comes out of the oven, quickly score it into pieces with a sharp knife and leave to cool in the pan.

These tasty treats also double up as a delicious offering for unexpected visitors. Keep a fresh batch handy in the cookie jar.

Sweet
Somethings

Perfect Preserves

If you want to create the perfect afternoon tea, you'll need a selection of lovely fruit preserves, or 'jams' as the British call them. And making your own just couldn't be more satisfying.

What is British jam?

Jam is a mixture of fruit and sugar cooked together until set. Pectin, a gum-like substance that occurs in varying amounts in the cell walls of fruit, is essential to setting. Acid is also necessary to help release the pectin, improve the color and flavor, and prevent crystallization. Fruits rich in pectin and acid are blackcurrants, cooking apples, crab apples, cranberries, damsons, gooseberries, lemons, limes, Seville oranges, quinces and redcurrants. Fruits containing a medium amount are dessert apples, apricots, bilberries, blackberries, greengages, loganberries, mulberries, plums and raspberries. Fruits low in pectin, which do not give a good set unless mixed with other high-pectin fruit, are cherries, elderberries, figs, grapes, japonica, medlars, nectarines, peaches, pears, rhubarb, rowanberries and strawberries. If acid is the only ingredient required and the fruit has enough pectin, the most convenient way of adding it is in the form of lemon, redcurrant or gooseberry juice.

To sterilize jars, bottles and lids

Wash in hot, soapy water or the dishwasher, making sure that there is no residue on them, and then rinse thoroughly in hot water. Sterilize using one of the following methods:

Stand the jars or bottles and lids right-side up on a wire rack in a large pan, making sure that they do not touch each other or the sides of the pan. Cover completely with water and then bring to a boil. Reduce the heat and simmer for 10 minutes and then remove from the water and stand upside down on a clean, thick cloth to drain. Dry completely in a preheated oven at 225°F, right-side up, on a baking sheet for about 15 minutes. They can be kept warm in the oven until required.

Preheat the oven to 350°F. Stand the jars, bottles and lids on the oven shelf and leave for 10 minutes to sterilize. Turn the oven off and keep them warm until ready to fill.

If your dishwasher has a very hot cycle, you can sterilize your jars, bottles and lids in that.

Jam is a classic accompaniment to scones

To make jam

Choosing and preparing the fruit

It should be dry, fresh and barely ripe. Over-ripe fruit does not set well as it is low in pectin.

Pick over the fruit, discarding any damaged parts, and wash or wipe it.

Simmer gently until soft and reduced by about one-third to break down the cell walls and release the pectin. Make sure that all fruit skins are completely soft, especially thick-skinned fruits such as blackcurrants, before adding the sugar, because this will instantly toughen them.

Choosing and using the sugar

There is no keeping difference between jams made with beet sugar and sugar cane.

Any kind of sugar (except confectioners' sugar) will make jam, but preserving sugar makes a slightly clearer jam which needs less stirring, and produces far less scum. Brown sugars can mask the fruit flavor.

Commercial jam sugar, based on granulated sugar with added pectin and acid, guarantees a set for any fruit. Choose the type that guarantees a set in 4 minutes with no testing. This is useful for low-pectin fruits but is rather expensive.

Warm the sugar in the oven before adding to the fruit to reduce the cooking time. Take the pan off the heat before adding the sugar and stir until completely dissolved.

If the mixture boils before the sugar is dissolved, it will crystallize and the jam will be crunchy and spoilt. Once the sugar is dissolved completely, bring the jam to a rolling boil (the boiling continues when the jam is stirred with a wooden spoon).

Testing for a set

Most jams reach setting point after 5–20 minutes' boiling, but always start testing for a set after 5 minutes as over-boiling spoils the color and flavor.

Saucer Test

Before you start making your jam, put a saucer into the refrigerator or freezer to get cold. Remove the jam from the heat and put about 2 tsp onto the cold saucer. Allow it to cool, then push your fingertip across the center of the jam. If the surface wrinkles well and the two halves remain separate, setting point has been reached. If not, return the pan to the heat and boil again for 5 minutes, then test again.

Temperature Test

If you have a sugar thermometer, hold it in the boiling jam, without resting it on the bottom of the pan. Bend over until your eyes are level with the 220°F mark on the thermometer: this is the temperature the jam should reach when it is at setting point.

Flake Test

To check setting point, do a quick 'flake' test. Dip the bowl of a cold wooden spoon in the jam. Take out and cool slightly, then let the jam drop from the edge of the spoon. At setting point, the jam runs together, forming flakes, which break off cleanly with a shake of the spoon.

Potting and covering

Wash the jars in very hot water and dry in the oven at 275°F. Leave them there until you are ready to pot the jam. The jars must be warmed before filling, or the hot jam will crack them.

Once the setting point has been reached, pot the jam immediately, except for strawberry and raspberry jam and all marmalades. Leave these to stand for 10–15 minutes to let the fruit or rind settle, to prevent it from rising to the surface in the jar.

Pour the jam into the jars using a ladle or small jug, filling them almost to the top, leaving no space for bacteria to grow. A jam funnel makes filling easier.

Cover the jam immediately with waxed paper discs, placing the waxed sides down on the surface of the preserve. The surface of the jam should be completely covered by the waxed paper (buy the right size for the type of jar used). Press gently to exclude all air. Then immediately add lids or dampened cellophane covers (damp side downwards) and secure with rubber bands.

✐ For every 3 lb sugar, the yield will be about 5 lb jam.

Storing

✐ Stand the jars of jam aside until completely cold, then label clearly with type of jam and the date it was made.

✐ Store in a cool, dark, dry and airy cupboard. Homemade jam and jam will keep well for up to one year, but may deteriorate in color and flavor if kept longer.

Strawberry jam

This is the jam everyone loves, young and old, and is the traditional one served with National Trust cream teas. It is only worth making if you have a good supply of fresh fruit from your own garden, or direct from a pick-your-own farm. This recipe will take several days, although it is very simple. Strawberries are lacking in acid and pectin, so choose small, firm berries, preferably of the more acid varieties, and use jam sugar to ensure a good set. If you have problems getting the jam to set, add the juice of 1 lemon when bringing the fruit and sugar to the boil.

3 lb 5 oz small strawberries
3 lb 5 oz jam sugar

1 Hull the strawberries, but do not wash them, and then layer with two-thirds of the sugar in a wide, shallow china or glass bowl. Sprinkle over the remaining sugar. Cover with a clean cloth and leave at room temperature (as long as your room is not too warm) for 24 hours.

2 Next day, scrape the contents of the bowl into a pan and bring slowly to the boil. Allow the mixture to bubble over a low heat for 5 minutes and then remove from the heat, cover with a clean cloth and leave for a further 48 hours.

3 Return the pan to the heat and bring back to the boil. Boil for about 10–15 minutes until setting point is reached (see page 243). Remove the pan from the heat and skim off any scum. Allow the jam to cool for 10 minutes and then give it a good stir, so that the fruit is well-dispersed—it will then remain suspended rather than rising to the top of the jam. Pot and cover in the usual way.

Apricot jam

Apricots need extra acid to give a good set, so lemon juice is added. It is especially good with freshly baked croissants.

3 lb fresh apricots
Juice of 1 lemon, strained
1¼ cups water
3 lb granulated sugar, warmed

1 Halve and stone the apricots, reserving 12 stones. Using a nutcracker, crack open the reserved stones and remove the kernels. Blanch them in boiling water for 1 minute, then drain and transfer to a bowl of cold water. Drain again, then rub off the skins with your fingers.

2 Simmer the apricots and kernels gently in the lemon juice and water for about 15 minutes or until the fruit is soft and the water has reduced. Add the warmed sugar and stir until it has completely dissolved, then boil rapidly for 10–15 minutes, or until setting point is reached (see page 243). Pot and cover in the usual way.

Raspberry jam

You need slightly under-ripe raspberries to make really successful jam with no hint of mustiness or mould, so if you do not grow your own raspberries, the next best thing is to find a pick-your-own farm. Loganberries can be used instead.

2¼ lb raspberries
2¼ lb granulated sugar

1 Pick over the raspberries carefully, but do not wash them. Put them in a large, shallow china or glass dish and pour over the sugar. Cover with a clean cloth and leave for 24 hours, pounding them together every now and again.

2 Next day, tip the raspberry and sugar mixture into a pan and bring very slowly to the boil, stirring frequently. Boil fast for 3–5 minutes, or until setting point is reached (see page 243). Pot and cover in the usual way.

High dumpsie dearie jam

Although an old Gloucestershire recipe, this jam was popular all over England in Victorian times, when it was called 'Mock Apricot Jam'.

2 lb cooking apples, peeled and cored
2 lb cooking pears, peeled and cored
2 lb large plums
Juice of 1 large lemon, strained
1¼ cups water
3 whole cloves
1 small cinnamon stick
6 lb granulated sugar, warmed

1 Cut the apples and pears into even-size pieces. Halve and stone the plums, reserving the stones, then place all the fruit in a large pan with the lemon juice and water. Tie the reserved plum stones, cloves and cinnamon in a piece of muslin and add to the fruit. Simmer very gently until the fruit is soft.

2 Remove and discard the muslin bag. Add the warmed sugar and stir until it has completely dissolved, then bring to a boil. Boil rapidly for about 15 minutes until setting point is reached (see page 243). Pot and cover in the usual way.

Cliveden red gooseberry & elderflower jam

A recipe used by the cooks at Cliveden's Conservatory Restaurant, just outside Maidenhead. Omit the elderflowers if you wish and substitute scented geranium leaves or other herbs.

3 lb gooseberries
1¼ cups water
6–8 elderflower heads
3 lb granulated sugar, warmed

1 Place the gooseberries in a large pan and add the water. Simmer the fruit gently for about 20 minutes, or until pulpy. Meanwhile, snip the tiny flowers off the elderflower heads, making sure they are clean and insect-free.

2 Stir the flowers and warmed sugar into the cooked fruit. Heat gently, stirring until the sugar has dissolved, and then boil rapidly for about 15 minutes until setting point is reached (see page 243). Pot and cover in the usual way.

Variations

Gooseberry & orange jam
Cook the gooseberries with the grated rind and juice of 3 oranges instead of the elderflowers.

Gooseberry & redcurrant jam
Use 2 lb gooseberries and 1 lb redcurrants and omit the elderflowers.

Gooseberry & rhubarb jam
Use 2 lb gooseberries and 1 lb chopped rhubarb. Cook the fruits separately to avoid overcooking the rhubarb. Omit the elderflowers.

Gooseberry & strawberry jam
Use 1½ lb gooseberries and 1½ lb strawberries. Cook the fruits separately to avoid overcooking the strawberries.
Omit the elderflowers.

Greengage & orange jam

Adding orange works very well with the subtle flavor of greengage jam.

2 lb greengages
1 large orange
½ lemon
2 lb granulated sugar, warmed

1 Wash the fruit and remove the stones, but reserve them. Put the fruit in a pan and tie the stones in a square of muslin. Add the muslin bag to the pan with the juice and thinly pared and sliced rind of the orange and lemon. Simmer gently for about 10 minutes or until the greengages are soft.

2 Stir in the warmed sugar and continue simmering gently, stirring continuously until the sugar has dissolved and then bring to a rolling boil. Boil for about 10 minutes until setting point is reached (see page 243). Remove from the heat and squeeze the muslin bag. Open it and crack some of the stones with a nutcracker; remove the kernels. Stir these kernels into the jam and then pot and cover in the usual way.

For Greengage, Orange and Walnut Jam, stir in ⅓ cup chopped walnuts after setting point is reached.

Blackcurrant jam

Blackcurrants make a gorgeously rich jam with a wonderful flavor, but make sure the initial cooking is thorough so that the skins are soft. Taste every now and again to check that the currants are well cooked before you add the sugar.

2 lb blackcurrants
2½ cups water
3 lb granulated sugar, warmed

1 Wash the currants and remove the strings and stalks. Place in a pan with the water and bring slowly to the boil. Reduce the heat and simmer gently for about 20 minutes, or until the fruit is tender, stirring occasionally.

2 Add the warmed sugar to the pan, stir until completely dissolved and then boil rapidly for about 5 minutes or until setting point is reached (see page 243). Pot and cover in the usual way.

Rhubarb & rose-petal jam

Use freshly picked, unsprayed, scented rose petals, red if possible, from the garden. Do not buy roses from a florist, as they will have been sprayed. Red roses give a better flavor and a lovely color.

1 lb rhubarb
Juice of 1 lemon
2¼ cups granulated sugar
2 handfuls of scented rose petals
(about 5 roses)

1 Wipe the rhubarb and cut into ½ in pieces. Put in a shallow china dish, add the lemon juice and then cover the rhubarb with the sugar. Cover with a clean cloth and leave to stand overnight.

2 Next day, remove the white bit, or heel, from each rose petal and discard. Cut the rose petals into strips and put in a pan with the rhubarb mixture. Bring to a boil slowly, stirring until the sugar has dissolved. Boil briskly until setting point is reached (see page 243). Leave to cool slightly and then pot and cover in the usual way.

Variations

Blackcurrant & rhubarb jam
Cook 1 lb rhubarb in 1¼ cups water until pulpy. In another pan cook 1 lb blackcurrants until tender. Mix the two fruits together and continue as above.

Blackcurrant & apple jam
Cook 12 oz peeled, cored and sliced apples in 1¼ cups water until tender. Add to the cooked blackcurrants and continue as above.

Conversion Charts

Conversions

Weight	Liquid measure	Length	Temperature
½ oz/10 g	1fl oz/30 ml	¼ in/0.5 cm	225°F, 110°C, gas mark ¼
1 oz/25 g	2fl oz/60 ml	½ in/1 cm	250°F, 120°C, gas mark ½
2 oz/60 g	3fl oz/85 ml	¾ in/1.5 cm	275°F, 140°C, gas mark 1
3 oz/85 g	4fl oz/120 ml	1 in/2.5 cm	300°F, 150°C, gas mark 2
4 oz/110 g	5fl oz/150 ml	2 in/5 cm	325°F, 170°C, gas mark 3
5 oz/140 g	10fl oz/300 ml	3 in/7.5 cm	350°F, 180°C, gas mark 4
6 oz/175 g	12fl oz/360 ml	4 in/10 cm	375°F, 190°C, gas mark 5
7 oz/200 g	15fl oz/450 ml	5 in/12.5 cm	400°F, 200°C, gas mark 6
8 oz/225 g	20fl oz/600 ml	6 in/15 cm	425°F, 220°C, gas mark 7
9 oz/250 g		7 in/17.5 cm	450°F, 230°C, gas mark 8
10 oz/280 g		8 in/20 cm	475°F, 240°C, gas mark 9
11 oz/310 g		9 in/22.5 cm	
12 oz/340 g		10 in/25 cm	
13 oz/370 g		11 in/27.5 cm	
14 oz/400 g		12 in/30 cm	
15 oz/425 g			
1 lb/450 g			
1½ lb/675 g			
2 lb/900 g			

**These approximate conversions are used throughout this book.
Use a standard cup for measuring.**

Cup measurements

Most ingredients in the recipes here are measured using cups, which come in standard sizes as detailed in the chart below. They are available online and from many specialist cookery retailers. If you do not have a set of baking cups see the chart on the next page. It is important to understand that when measuring in cups it is the volume of an ingredient that's measured, not the weight. A cup of icing sugar will weigh less than a cup of soft brown sugar, for example, even though they are the same volume. Therefore when converting make sure that you have looked up the conversion for your particular ingredient.

Ingredient	oz per 1 cup	grams per 1 cup	Ingredient	oz per 1 cup	grams per 1 cup
Almonds, flaked	4	110	Jam	11	310
Almonds, ground	3½	100	Margarine	8	225
Breadcrumbs	2	60	Marmalade	11	310
Cake crumbs	2	60	Mincemeat	11	310
Candied peel, mixed	5	140	Muesli	5	140
Carrot, grated	4	110	Nuts, roughly chopped	4	110
Cheese, cream	8	225	Oatmeal	6	175
Cheese, curd	8	225	Plums, chopped	7	200
Cheese, grated	4	110	Porridge oats	3	85
Cocoa	4	110	Raisins	6	175
Coconut, shredded	3½	100	Rice	7	200
Cornflour	5	140	Rolled oats	3	85
Cream, double	8	225	Semolina	7	200
Crème fraiche	8	225	Sesame seeds	4	110
Currants	5	140	Sorghum flour	4	110
Dates, chopped	5	140	Sugar, caster	8	225
Dried apricots	6	175	Sugar, dark muscovado	6	175
Drinking chocolate	4	110	Sugar, Demerara	7	200
Figs, chopped	7	200	Sugar, granulated	8	225
Flour, rice	5	140	Sugar, icing	4	110
Flour, white	5	140	Sugar, soft brown	7	200
Flour, wholemeal	6	175	Sultanas	6	175
Glace cherries	7	200	Syrup, golden	12	340
			Treacle, black	12	340

Fractions of cups to weights

Use this chart to convert fractions of cups to weights, but be sure to use the correct conversion for your ingredient (see previous page).

1 cup = 2 oz

	¼ cup	½ oz
	½ cup	1 oz
	¾ cup	1½ oz

1 cup = 3 oz

	¼ cup	¾ oz
	⅓ cup	1 oz
	½ cup	1½ oz
	⅔ cup	2 oz
	¾ cup	2¼ oz

1 cup = 3 ½ oz

scant	¼ cup	1 oz
	⅓ cup	1¼ oz
	½ cup	1¾ oz
	⅔ cup	2⅓ oz
	¾ cup	2¾ oz
generous	1 cup	4 oz
	2¼ cups	8 oz

1 cup = 4 oz

	¼ cup	1 oz
	⅓ cup	1⅓ oz
	½ cup	2 oz
	⅔ cup	2⅔ oz
	¾ cup	3 oz

1 cup = 5 oz

	¼ cup	1¼ oz
	⅓ cup	1⅔ oz
	½ cup	2½ oz
	⅔ cup	3⅓ oz
	¾ cup	3¾ oz
generous	¾ cup	4 oz
	1¼ cups	6 oz

	1⅓ cups	6½ oz
	1½ cups	7½ oz
	1⅔ cups	8 oz
	1 ¾ cups	9 oz
	2 cups	10 oz
	2¼ cups	11 oz
	2⅓ cups	12 oz
	3¼ cups	1 lb

1 cup = 6 oz

	¼ cup	1½ oz
	⅓ cup	2 oz
	½ cup	3 oz
	⅔ cup	4 oz
	¾ cup	4½ oz

1 cup = 7 oz

	¼ cup	1¾ oz
	⅓ cup	2 oz
	½ cup	3½ oz
	⅔ cup	4 oz
	¾ cup	5¼ oz
generous	¾ cup	6 oz

1 cup = 8 oz

	¼ cup	2 oz
	⅓ cup	2⅔ oz
	½ cup	4 oz
	⅔ cup	5⅓ oz
	¾ cup	6 oz

1 cup = 11 oz

	¼ cup	2¾ oz
	½ cup	5½ oz
	¾ cup	8¼ oz

1 cup = 12 oz

	¼ cup	3 oz
	⅓ cup	4 oz
	½ cup	6 oz
	⅔ cup	8 oz
	¾ cup	9 oz

British equivalents for ingredients

The ingredients and measurements used in this book are in American English. Use the information here for British equivalents.

US term	British term
All-purpose flour	Plain flour
Baking sheet	Baking tray
Bittersweet chocolate	Dark chocolate
Broiler / broil	Grill
Cake pan	Cake tin
Chocolate callets	Chocolate buttons
Confectioners' sugar	Icing sugar
Cookie	Biscuit
Corn syrup	Golden syrup
cornstarch	Cornflour
Cupcake liners	Cupcake cases
Decorating bag	Piping bag
Frosting	Icing
Golden raisins	Sultanas
Heavy cream	Double cream
Jellyroll	Swiss roll
Layer cake pan	Sandwich pan
molasses	Black treacle
Mold	Mould
Muffin pans	Muffin trays
Parchment paper	Baking paper
Self-rising flour	Self-raising flour
Semisweet chocolate	Plain chocolate
Shortening	Lard
Store	Shop
Superfine sugar	Caster sugar
White bread flour	Strong white flour
Whole-wheat	Wholemeal
Wholefood	Health food
Zucchini	Courgette

Anova Books would like to thank Kate Shirazi, Emma Goss-Custard for the use of recipes from the following books: Baking Magic, Cake Magic, Cookie Magic, Cupcake Magic, Muffin Magic, and Honeybuns Gluten-Free Baking.

We would also like to thank the National Trust for the kind use of their text and recipes from the following books: Countrywise Cook Book, Good Old Fashioned Teatime Baking, Good Old Fashioned Jams Pickles and Preserves, and Tea Classified.

Index